BRILLIANT QUESTIONS ABOUT GROWING UP

PUFFIN BOOKS

UK | USA | Canada | Ireland | Australia
India | New Zealand | South Africa

Puffin Books is part of the Penguin Random House group of companies
whose addresses can be found at global.penguinrandomhouse.com.

www.penguin.co.uk
www.puffin.co.uk
www.ladybird.co.uk

First published 2020

001

Text design by Sally Griffin

Printed and bound in China

A CIP catalogue record for this book is available from the British Library

ISBN: 978–0–241–44798–7

All correspondence to:
Puffin Books
Penguin Random House Children's
One Embassy Gardens, 8 Viaduct Gardens, London SW11 7BW

AMY FORBES-ROBERTSON
& ALEX FRYER

BRILLIANT QUESTIONS ABOUT GROWING UP

SIMPLE ANSWERS ABOUT BODIES AND BOUNDARIES

ILLUSTRATED BY AVA PUCKETT

PUFFIN

INTRODUCTION

Welcome to this book filled with **brilliant** questions and awesome answers to help you understand **AMAZING** things like:

- How the body works
- How babies are made, grown and born
- How to talk about families, friendships and feelings
- Things that might happen when children grow up into adults

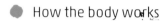

You might want to read this whole book in one go. Or you can just find the right bits when you need them! You might have a particular question about something, so you can use the contents page to find the part you're interested in. You can read the chapters in any order, and if there's a word you haven't seen before, there's a helpful glossary at the back to help you understand.

You could read this book on your own, or you could read it with a trusted adult and together have some really great conversations about these topics. You might even have a giggle too – because some of it is a little bit funny!

GROWN-UPS, TURN TO PAGE 105!

CONTENTS

CHAPTER 1

HUMAN BODIES

Bodies are **BRILLIANT**.

We all have them, they come in all different shapes and sizes, they change as we get older, and it is really useful to understand what they do (even though they are often covered with clothes).

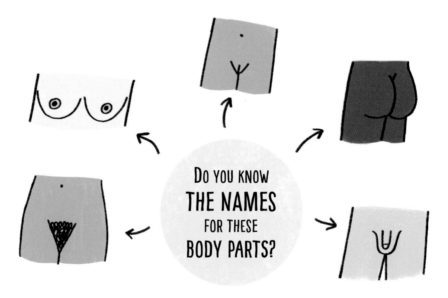

DO YOU KNOW
THE NAMES
FOR THESE
BODY PARTS?

Throughout this book, we use the proper words for things. And yes – knowing the different names for our body parts is really important! Of course, you can carry on saying words like *fanny* or *woo-woo* or *flower* or *willy* or *winkie* or *noodle* if that's what you want to do, but we don't use different words for our noses or hands or eyes,

so **why** should we treat our genitals any DIFFERENTLY?

If you ever need to talk about your genitals, or ask a doctor or a nurse for help, then it's good to know the real words. If you went to see a doctor and said,

I've got an ouch on my **tootsie**

the doctor isn't going to know what you are talking about! But if you can explain that you fell off your scooter and hurt your big toe, and there is a sore bit just under your toenail that really stings . . . then the doctor is going to be able to help you more easily.

The more we understand our bodies and know the right words, the more power we have to look after them. So the words **nipples**, **breasts**, **penis**, **testicles**, **scrotum**, **vulva**, **labia** and **clitoris** may be quite new to you, but they're extremely useful words to know.

Let's start with **BOTTOMS** . . .

Bottom is a pretty hilarious word, as is *bum*, *backside*, *rear end*, or *derrière* if you're feeling fancy. But no matter what you call it, your bottom is really important to learn about.

I bet you LAUGHED!

You will already be quite familiar with how your bottom works because most people use it all the time. Bottoms are great padding for our bones, and for the majority of people they are very useful for getting *waste materials* out of our bodies.

YES, WE ARE TALKING ABOUT POO . . .

A bottom consists of **buttocks** and an **anus**. The buttocks are the two round, squidgy bits we sit on, and the anus is the hole between them where the poo comes out that leads to the **bowel**.

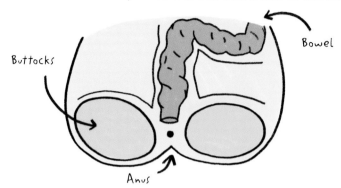

Bowel

Buttocks

Anus

It's important to make an effort to keep our anus clean so that it stays healthy.

Bottoms come in different shapes and sizes. Some are very squishy, some are bony, some are peachy, and some are hairy.

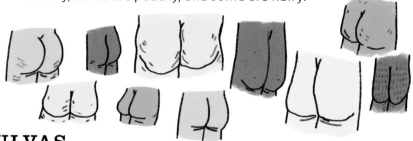

VULVAS

You might not have heard the word **vulva** before, but it is the correct name for these external genitals. Babies with vulvas are usually called 'female' when they are born. If you have a vulva, you could look in the mirror if you're interested to see what it looks like, or here is a picture of its parts.

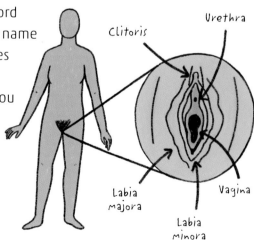

Clitoris

Urethra

Labia majora

Labia minora

Vagina

Inside, there are folds of skin called **labia**, and at the top of the labia is a **clitoris**, which is very sensitive and full of tickly nerve endings. Most of the clitoris is hidden behind the skin, but you can just see the tip of it at the top of the vulva. Below the clitoris is a teeny-tiny hole called a **urethra**, which is where the wee comes out and leads to the **bladder**, where the wee comes from. This is different from a second hole called the **vagina**, which is not for wee but leads to the internal genitals called the **cervix**, the **womb**, the **fallopian tubes** and the **ovaries**.

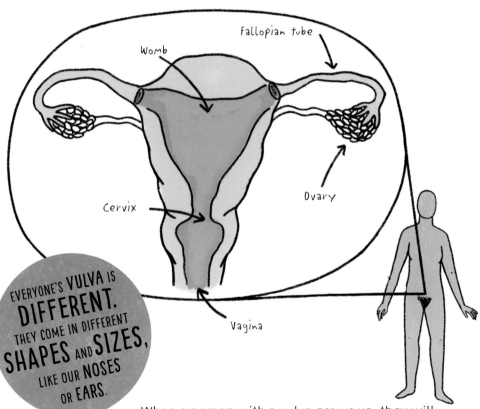

Womb

Fallopian tube

Cervix

Ovary

Vagina

EVERYONE'S **VULVA** IS **DIFFERENT.** THEY COME IN DIFFERENT **SHAPES** AND **SIZES,** LIKE OUR **NOSES** OR **EARS**.

When a person with a vulva grows up, they will probably get some pubic hair on the vulva area too. You might have seen this on a family member in the shower, or on people at the swimming pool, or maybe you have never seen anyone naked, which is OK too.

PENIS

The **penis** and **testicles** are these external genitals. Babies with them are usually called 'male' when they are born.

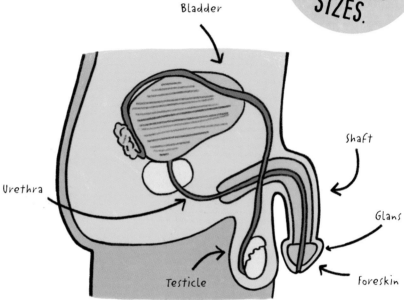

Bladder

Shaft

Urethra

Glans

Testicle

Foreskin

The penis has a **shaft** and a head that is called the **glans**. Wee comes out of the hole at the tip of the glans. The hole is the opening of the **urethra**, which is linked to the **bladder**, where the wee is stored.

There is often a roll of skin called a **foreskin** that covers the glans. Most males find that their foreskin stays covering the tip of the penis for the first few years of life. At around the age of three to five years, the foreskin can separate from the glans. This is nothing dramatic – it just pulls back a bit so that you can see what is underneath the foreskin, and it means that the penis is a bit easier to keep clean. If the foreskin hasn't detached, you don't need to worry. It might just happen a bit later on.

Some people with penises are **circumcised**. This means that part or all of the foreskin has been removed. It is usually done by doctors and can be for medical, cultural or religious reasons. It changes how a penis looks a little bit, but it doesn't usually change how a penis behaves or what it feels like.

It's typical for penises to change quite a lot – sometimes they are soft and downward-facing, and other times become a bit bigger and stand to attention, which is called an **erection**.

Erections can be **out of your control,** a bit like a yawn or a sneeze, and they **ALWAYS** go back down again in the end.

The testicles sit at the base of the penis, and are two little grape-sized balls called **testes** covered in a sack of skin called a **scrotum**. Inside the scrotum is some fluid to protect the testes.

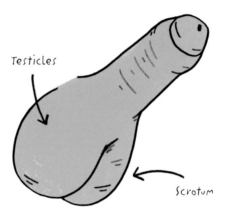

Testicles

Scrotum

The penis and the testicles are very **SENSITIVE,** so if you are the owner of this body part, you need to be gentle with them and take **good care** of them.

When a person with a penis becomes grown-up, they will probably get some pubic hair on the area round the base of the penis. Perhaps you've already noticed this, or it is also perfectly fine if you have never seen pubic hair before.

BREASTS

Breasts – which you might know as *boobs*, *boobies* or something else – are visible on the outside of the chest, and look like this.

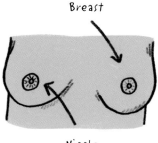

Even though there are usually two, they don't tend to be a matching pair – more like sisters than twins. They are very different on each person.

PEOPLE HAVE **BIG ONES**, SMALL ONES, **ROUND** ONES, LONG ONES, POINTY ONES – THERE IS **NO ONE NORMAL WAY** FOR THEM TO LOOK.

One of the reasons bodies have breasts is for creating milk to feed babies. Milk is produced in the **milk ducts** and **lobes**, which are on the inside of the breast, and it comes out through the **nipple**.

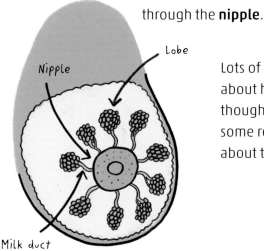

Lots of children are curious about how breasts work, so we thought we would answer some really common questions about them.

We'll answer questions throughout this book about lots of **different things**, but if you want to know **MORE**, you can always ask one of your **trusted adults**. A trusted adult is someone who you feel **safe** talking to, who wants to help you and who you think will give you honest advice – someone like a **parent**, **carer**, **doctor** or **teacher**.

If you don't feel that there are people in your life you can trust, then you can turn to page 104 for a list of organizations that you can ask for help.

● How does the milk get in if you have a baby?

If a body grows a baby, it usually creates a fluid called breast milk, which is filled with nutrients to feed the baby. In the same way a body makes blood and skin and bones, it makes its own milk. The really clever part is that the body changes what is in the milk depending on what the baby needs.

Some parents don't have breasts and some people don't create their own milk, or have a tricky time feeding their babies. There are other ways of getting milky drinks for your baby, like going to the doctor's or the shops to buy special baby milk. Sometimes people who create breast milk give it to hospitals for poorly babies or for people who can't feed their baby with their own milk.

● How does the milk actually come out?

The baby 'latches on' by filling its mouth with the breast so that the tip of the nipple is right at the back of the baby's mouth. Then the baby's jaw starts to move up and down, and the milk starts to flow. It doesn't come out of the nipple like a tap, it comes out like a shower, with lots of little holes squirting in different directions.

● If I suck a nipple now, will milk come out?

If a body produces breast milk, this milk usually stops being produced when the baby stops **breastfeeding**. It's called **supply** and **demand**, which means that, if the baby stops asking for milk, the breast stops producing it. This might happen when babies begin to eat solid food.

This mostly happens between the ages of six months and two years, but some children breastfeed for much longer.

● **What if you can't see the baby during the day to breastfeed?**

If an adult is doing the breastfeeding, then they can't be away from the baby for very long, but there are other ways to get the milk out. One way is to pump it out and save it in the fridge or freezer. This is called **expressing** the milk, and you can put it in a bottle so that another person can feed the baby. Or a family can choose to buy a special type of baby milk that is sold in shops.

● **Why do boys have nipples?**

When an embryo is growing in the womb for the first few weeks, it isn't clear if it has a female body or a male body yet. The nipples are formed in these first few weeks when an embryo is really, really tiny. Everyone starts with them, just in case they're needed! Some babies go on to grow actual breasts that may be able to make breast milk one day, and the other babies don't – but they keep their nipples anyway.

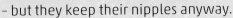

● Why do some boobs wobble more than others?
Breasts come in lots of different shapes and sizes, and sometimes bigger ones might be a bit wobblier. It also depends on whether people are wearing bras or not. Tight clothes or not. Running or sitting still.

Everyone makes **different** choices depending on their bodies, lives, jobs, BELIEFS, **religions** and CULTURES.

● Why did that person say 'OUCH' when I bumped into their chest? I didn't mean to! It was an accident!
Sometimes breasts are a bit painful and can feel different at different times. Bits of us can feel more sensitive or tender at different ages and stages. With breasts, it's not usually something to worry about, because it's typical if they change a lot in a week or a month or a year or a whole lifetime. So if you crash into a tender breast and the owner of that breast yelps and yells

OUCH!

don't worry too much, and make sure to say sorry. It's always important to listen if someone lets you know that they've been hurt.

CHAPTER 2

WHERE
DO WE ALL
COME FROM?

You probably know a bit about how **life cycles** and **REPRODUCTION** work in nature. It isn't all that different when it comes to humans.

There are **SEEDS**.

There are **EGGS**.

There are **BABIES**.

There are growing **FAMILIES**.

WE AREN'T **EMBARRASSED** TO TALK ABOUT THESE TOPICS FOR PLANTS AND ANIMALS, SO IT DOESN'T HAVE TO BE **WEIRD** OR **CONFUSING** TO TALK ABOUT HOW THEY WORK FOR **HUMANS**.

There are different ways to get a baby inside a person's tummy, so it's important never to assume how a baby was made. There are, however, a few things that you always need for it to work.

You need an egg.

You need a sperm.

And you need a womb to grow the baby in.

Now, let's talk about what an egg and a sperm are, exactly.

And no – the egg isn't like ones that you've seen in the supermarket. These eggs inside a human are round and approximately the same size as a speck of dust – you can just about see them with the human eye.

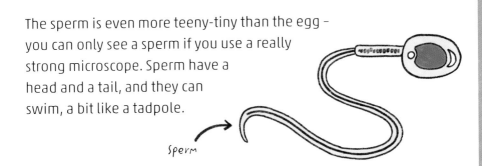

Ovary filled with eggs

Egg

This female baby is born with lots of little eggs already inside them. There are up to two million eggs combined across both ovaries, which is where the eggs stay until the body matures into an adult and starts releasing them into the fallopian tubes.

The sperm is even more teeny-tiny than the egg – you can only see a sperm if you use a really strong microscope. Sperm have a head and a tail, and they can swim, a bit like a tadpole.

Sperm

When this male baby is born, they don't have any sperm. Their testicles begin to create sperm when they are maturing into an adult.

To make a baby, the egg and sperm need to come together. There are different ways to make this happen. Sometimes it's when two humans both agree that they want to make a baby together, and then they can do something called **sexual intercourse** – sex for short. This process is also sometimes called **reproduction**. This is when they both choose to connect the sperm and the egg together with their bodies.

This can happen when the erect penis enters the vagina to deliver the sperm to the egg. Millions of sperm are released in a creamy white fluid called **semen**, and one of them might join up with an egg. If it does, this is called **fertilization**.

Sperm

Egg

The joined-up egg and sperm may grow into an **embryo** inside the womb, which may go on to grow into a **foetus**. And this foetus may grow into a baby.

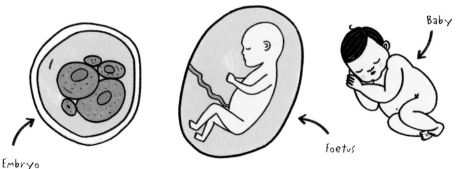

Embryo

Foetus

Baby

BUT this is only **one way** of making a baby.

Sometimes eggs and sperm don't connect when adults want them to, and a doctor or nurse can help them connect. Sometimes people with eggs have the sperm inserted into their body by a medical professional. Sometimes people are single or don't have sperm or eggs which can grow into a baby. Someone they know, or someone they don't know, might **donate** their sperm or eggs to them.

At other times, doctors can put an egg and a sperm in a little dish so that they connect and begin to grow an embryo. This process is called **in vitro fertilization**, which is a VERY long name – most people call it **IVF** for short. This embryo can then be put into a womb to grow. The womb might belong to a parent or it might belong to someone else. If it belongs to someone else, that person usually calls themselves a **surrogate**. This means they grow the baby in their body.

● **Can you eat the sperm to get it into your tummy?**
No, you don't eat the sperm. If you ate the sperm, it would end up in your stomach, where your food goes, and then it would come out as wee or poo.

Babies **don't** grow in stomachs.
They grow in **WOMBS**.

● **Why do some children look like their parents?**
Some people do and some people don't. The egg and sperm that made you had lots of information about the people who produced them, which is how your appearance is decided. If you look at your family, you may just see some connections with the colour of your hair or the colour of your eyes, your height, or if you have freckles. Lots of people don't look like the rest of their family for many different reasons. Having different hair or skin tones doesn't make them any less your family. So it's OK if you aren't exactly like your parents or siblings! The information about how you look comes from the egg and the sperm that made you.

But you are also unique. One of a kind. **Just you.**

● What happens if both parents have sperm or both parents have eggs?

Let's talk about **sexuality**,
which means **WHO** people are attracted to.
Sexuality might stay the same for someone's
whole life, or it might **change**.

If you are a woman and you are only attracted to and fall in love with a man, or if you are a man and you are only attracted to and fall in love with a woman, you would probably use the word **heterosexual** to describe yourself.

You might have heard the words **lesbian**, **gay** or **bisexual**. We are going to explain what these words mean because it's difficult to understand relationships if we don't understand relationship words.

If you are a woman and you are only attracted to other women, we can use the word *lesbian*. But not all women who love women will use that word. They might call themselves gay or use any other word they choose, because if it is about you, then *you* get to decide what is right for *you*.

If you are a man and you are only attracted to other men, you may choose to use the word *gay*. *You're* the one who gets to decide what you want to call yourself.

If you are a person who is attracted to both men and women, then you might call yourself *bisexual*. This doesn't necessarily mean that you would have a boyfriend and a girlfriend at the same time. It means that you feel comfortable being in a romantic relationship with men or women.

When some people talk about **sexuality** they might talk about *plus*, or use a + symbol. This is to show that there are lots **more** sexualities and ways to talk about them than the ones we've mentioned here.

NOW, BACK TO THE QUESTION ABOUT **BOTH PARENTS** HAVING SPERM OR HAVING EGGS ...

If two people with sperm want to make a baby, they can certainly do that. They might use their own sperm and be given an egg from someone. They could ask a surrogate parent with a womb to grow their baby for them. And if two people with eggs want to make a baby, they can be given some sperm from someone and use one of their own eggs, and perhaps one of them could use their womb to grow the baby.

● **Are there other ways of getting a baby?**
Some people don't use their sperm or eggs and they instead **adopt** a baby. If you are adopted, this means that you don't live with your **birth parents** (the people who provided the sperm and egg) – you have a new person or family who take care of you. People who choose to adopt choose to welcome a child into their lives and bring that person up as part of their family. Some people do this because it is the only way they can have a family, but others may choose to adopt for a range of other reasons, such as wanting to share their life with a child who doesn't have a home.

There is also something called **fostering**. This is when people look after a child for a certain amount of time to help out, usually because the birth family aren't able to. Sometimes it's because the birth family needs a break and foster parents can give them the support they need. You can foster or adopt babies and children from other countries and cultures too. Your family can grow and grow and grow in many different ways.

● Can I have a baby now?

No, not yet. Having a baby is a very grown-up thing to do. The law says you have to be at least sixteen years old to have sex. And your body needs to go through lots of changes that happen gradually over a long period of time before it is ready to reproduce. Your body doesn't start having eggs and sperm that work until it starts maturing. Girls are usually born with all of their tiny eggs inside them, but they don't work in the right way for baby-making until a child's body has turned into an adult's body. Boys' bodies don't usually start producing sperm and storing it in their testicles until their child body has become more like an adult body. It is also a huge responsibility having a family (ask any parent!) so best to leave it until you are much more able to look after a baby.

**What do you think the qualities you need
to LOOK AFTER a baby are?**

I am a twin. How does that work?

Twins can happen in different ways. To make **non-identical twins** (who look different) you need two eggs and two sperm to both connect and make two different embryos. To make **identical twins** (twins  who look pretty much exactly the same) you have one egg and one sperm that connect to form one embryo. That embryo divides in two and both halves go on to become their own whole person – an exact matching pair because they were made from the same sperm and the same egg. Identical twins are always born both male or  both female, but are still unique people with individual personalities. One of the identical twins could LOVE ice cream, but the other might think that it's disgusting.

And did you know that one twin is always born first?

This means that one twin is older, even if only by a minute or two.

If you have two children, does that mean that you have sex two times?

Actually, there is another thing about sex . . . It's not just a way of connecting a sperm and an egg. It is also a way of showing your love or affection for the other person in a grown-up, romantic relationship. It's exciting. And fun. And feels nice. Some people like to hold hands, some people hug, some people kiss, some people choose to connect with each other with their whole bodies.

Sex is often part of a mature **RELATIONSHIP** and happens between people who have decided to **share** their bodies with each other.

Sex can feel great for both people. Sometimes people call it *making love* because they are using their bodies to show their love.

Some people do this thing called sex or making love quite a lot, NOT to make a baby, but to enjoy each other and have fun because they like how it feels. If one person has sperm and one person has eggs, then there are clever ways of making sure that they don't connect if you don't want them to. If this is something you choose to do in the future then you can talk to a doctor or nurse about the best options for *you*.

● Where does sex actually happen?
Anywhere, when both grown-ups have agreed that they are happy to connect their bodies. It's a very personal thing, so it's important for people to share their feelings about it and respect each other. Usually they take their clothes off to do this and it can take a bit of time, so it's sensible to be somewhere private, warm and comfy like a bed, but it's up to them to decide.

● What time do you do sex?
Again, it's up to the grown-ups involved! Daytime, night-time, morning, evening, winter, autumn, spring or summer. If both people have listened to each other's feelings and are happy with the choice, then it is the right time!

● Does everyone do it?
No, not everyone. Some people might choose not to have sex ever because they don't want to. Some people love having sex, while some people are not that bothered at all. Others might wait until they are married. There are some rules about it too. In the UK the law says that both people must be over sixteen years old so that they understand the choice they are making.

Everyone involved **MUST** make their own choice and agree, so that it's **equal** and kind and FUN for everyone.

So, if you're old enough, taking care of each other and working it out together, then it doesn't matter who you are. Older people, shorter people, taller people, blind people, grandparents, married people, people with diabetes, single people, people with disabilities, pregnant people, people in wheelchairs, students, people with mental illness, business people, famous people, people with arthritis, teachers or celebrities . . . Pretty much anyone!

What if I want to know more?

It's totally fine to want to know more about all of this. There will be lots of lessons as you go through school, but if you're really keen to know more, you can ask adults, such as parents, teachers and doctors about it. Nature and science are all around us, so it's great to ask lots of questions that will help you understand the bits of the world you are interested in.

CHAPTER 3

FROM PREGNANCY TO BEING BORN

You probably know what being **PREGNANT** is from how people look on the **OUTSIDE**.

If someone you know has told you that they're going to have a baby, then has, over nine months, grown a big round belly and maybe developed strange cravings for foods that you think are GROSS, like sausages dipped in strawberry jam, that means they're pregnant!

What you might **NOT** know is what is happening to a pregnant person on the **inside**.

Once an embryo is inside the womb, it can grow into a foetus, and a foetus can grow into a baby. Sometimes this might not work out for all sorts of reasons and it won't grow into a baby. If it does work out, the foetus needs to be given food and water from the pregnant body so that it keeps growing and growing. There is this incredible tube called the **umbilical cord** that feeds the baby. It links the baby to the pregnant person's body through a **placenta**, which is how all the food and oxygen is moved from one place to the other.

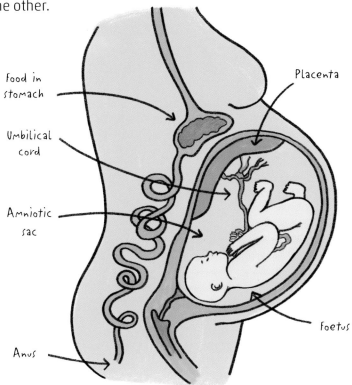

Food in stomach

Placenta

Umbilical cord

Amniotic sac

Foetus

Anus

Bodies can move around to make space for the baby while the baby is growing. The ribs move up, the hips move outwards and the stomach is squished out of the way.

If everything works properly, the baby gets

bigger and bigger and **BIGGER**

inside the womb, starting off as small as a teeny-weeny piece of rice and growing to reach the weight of a watermelon. Ears and fingers and lungs and hair and a tongue and teeth and everything else all grow inside the womb. So many changes happen gradually to the foetus, taking it from a tiny ball of cells to a baby.

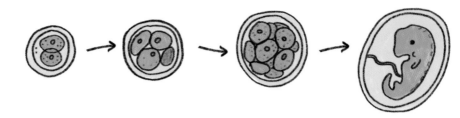

- At **SIX WEEKS** it has a tail and looks like a tadpole.

- At **TWELVE WEEKS** it can suck its thumb.

- At **FOURTEEN WEEKS** it can wee.

- At **SIXTEEN WEEKS** it can form a fist and have facial expressions.

- At **NINETEEN** weeks it starts to kick.

- At **TWENTY-THREE WEEKS** it can practise breathing (even though it can't actually use its lungs properly yet).

- At **TWENTY-FIVE WEEKS** it can get hiccups.

- At **TWENTY-SIX WEEKS** it can blink and respond to light; if you shine a torch in its direction, it may squirm.

- At **THIRTY-TWO** weeks its eyes can focus.

- At **THIRTY-FOUR** weeks it can recognize voices and music.

- At **THIRTY-EIGHT** weeks it has a big poo, called **meconium**, inside its body, waiting to come out once it is born.

- At **THIRTY-NINE** week its head should be facing downwards, ready to be born.

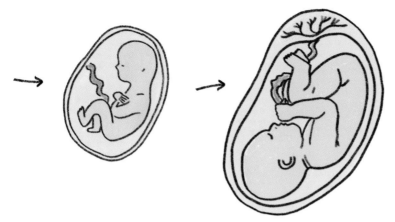

Pregnancy usually takes about forty weeks, or nine months, but this isn't exact and some babies come out before or after this. If a baby is born early, before thirty-seven weeks, it is called **premature** and the doctors can help look after it until it is big and strong enough to go home.

Sometimes the baby just needs a bit more time inside the womb and will naturally be born **late**, or doctors and midwives can help the baby get out.

If the body is ready when the time comes, it goes into **labour**, which means it starts working to push the baby down. The baby is squeezed down out of the womb, through the cervix, through the vaginal opening and into the world.

But this is only one birth story. Babies can be born in lots of different ways.

DO YOU KNOW **HOW YOU** WERE **BORN?**

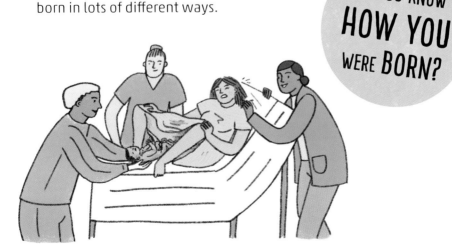

● Am I allowed to ask how I was born?

Have you ever asked your family about your birth story? They might be able to tell you. Birth can happen in lots of different ways, and different religions or cultures or families will have different stories to share. Who was there at your birth? How long did it take? So yes, ask away . . . You might find out some really interesting and exciting things. But not every family will want to talk about it.

● What are belly buttons for?

Everyone has a belly button. You might have an *innie*, an *outie* or an *inbetweenie*, and you might have some questions about how it got there.

When a baby is born, it is still connected to the placenta by the umbilical cord, but as soon as the baby is out of the womb and in the world it can breathe its own oxygen and drink its own milk – so it doesn't really need the placenta or umbilical cord any more.

The placenta needs to come out of the body that has just given birth and, at some point, someone must clamp and cut the cord.

This disconnects the baby's body from the placenta. It might sound scary, but it doesn't hurt anyone at all! The last little bit of cord stays attached to a newborn baby for a few days, then just falls off, a bit like a scab. And what's left?

Voilà, it's a belly button!

Do you know who cut your cord? Was it one of your parents, a family member, a family friend, a doctor, a midwife or a nurse? Your family might be happy to tell you more if you ask them.

● **How does the baby's head fit out of such a small hole?**
The very small vaginal opening has the power to stretch to make room for the baby as it comes out. Once the squeezing and the stretching is nearly done and the baby is almost out, it takes one final squeeze, push and stretch (which can be HARD work) for the slippery baby to slide out. Afterwards, the vagina hole usually goes back to how it used to be. The big tummy will go back in eventually, the ribs will move back down and the stomach will go back to where it was before the baby moved in. Some things might permanently change, like being left with stretch marks, wider hips or different-shaped breasts, but most bodies are really strong and find a way to put themselves back together again! For some people this new body takes a while to get used to, and for others they LOVE their new body and are really proud of it.

● **Someone told me that babies are all gooey and bloody when they come out? Is that true?**
Yes . . . because they have been on the inside, which is all gooey and bloody. The womb is a bit like a water balloon and full of a special sort of watery fluid called **amniotic fluid**, which keeps the baby safe. When a baby is born, this fluid must come out too. In the goo and blood there are loads of lovely good germs and bacteria that help the baby stay healthy, so it's not gross or dirty, but in fact a very good thing.

● **Can you be born in water?**
Yes, there are lots of different ways of being born. At home, in a hospital, in the taxi on the way to hospital, in an ambulance or in a

birth pool full of water. Some people give birth standing up, sitting down or even crawling around on the floor. Lying down on a bed is usually the way we see it in films or on TV, but that doesn't reflect everyone's story. Sometimes it can take a long time; sometimes it can be really quick; some people are quiet and peaceful; some people are shouty; some people love it; some people don't; some people find it easier than others; some people find it tough. It's incredibly different for everyone.

● My parents told me I was born by a caesarean. What's that?

There are lots of reasons for babies to be born in hospitals or with doctors there to help, just in case. If the baby isn't finding its own way out, it might need some help, or people might plan to give birth this way. Doctors cut an opening in the tummy and the baby comes out that way, using medicine so that it doesn't hurt. This way of being born is called a **C-section** or **caesarean**.

● I have a disability. Was I like that before I was born?

When the sperm and the egg connect, they create a unique person – even the most identical twins in the world have different fingerprints. Sometimes people might have a special type of body or a special type of brain. Maybe they will be a very small person who will never grow to be very tall, or someone who can't walk or someone who can't talk. Maybe they will grow differently in the womb and end up with one hand being smaller than the other. They could get poorly inside the womb and this changes how their brain works. They might come into the world not being able to see or hear or poo.

Sometimes the doctors can help with this and sometimes that is just the way that person is going to be forever. Others change as they grow up and they might get an illness, or a part of their body starts working differently. There are as many different disabilities as there are different people. Every human will have their own story and you can ask your family if you want to know more about yours.

⬤ I don't know how I was born . . .

That's OK. Some people will never know how they were born. This might be because they are adopted, fostered or in care and don't know their birth parents, or it might just be that the person who gave birth to you doesn't want to talk about it yet or maybe ever.

For some people, the day they gave birth was one of the best in their life, like being a superhero! Giving birth can be such an amazing thing that sometimes people cry because they feel overwhelmed with emotion. For other people, however, giving birth might have been a difficult or painful experience, and they may not like to talk about it. That's OK too.

If you don't know your birth story – don't worry. Maybe one day you will give birth, or you may be lucky enough to be there when someone else does.

⬤ Does everyone have to have babies when they grow up?

Absolutely not! Some people might love to have children, but find it tricky to make and grow and give birth to a baby. Others might not plan a baby and then end up getting one by accident. Or if someone gets pregnant without meaning to, they might choose to get help from a doctor or nurse to stop the pregnancy leading to a baby.

Lots of people choose not to have a family at all or might not want to be in a relationship with another person. They might be very content as a one! Or they could be a two and not want to change that. Or they might want lots of different partners during their lifetime. Some people are very happy with just nieces and nephews or cats or hamsters. They might even think that there are already enough babies and children in the world. Everyone is different and can choose what's right for them.

● Who can I ask about all of this?

If your parent or someone you know is having a baby, it's natural to be curious. They might take you along to see the doctors, midwives and nurses, and you can ask these medical professionals any questions you have – they are usually very kind and happy to talk about what they do. If you're worried about the idea of giving birth, then don't be. This isn't something you would do for a very long time and you can decide much later whether you would like to give birth.

If you do know someone who is pregnant, they may show you a picture of their baby INSIDE THE WOMB! This is taken with a special camera and is called an **ultrasound**. In an ultrasound you can see an outline of a baby and you can also tell if there are twins or triplets! Sometimes people choose to find out the **sex** of their baby from one of these pictures, which they may really want to know, or they could want a total surprise, or it might not matter to them. But what does that actually mean?

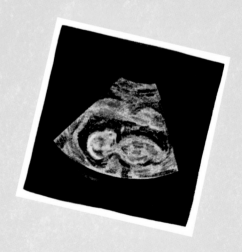

CHAPTER 4

SEX AND GENDER

WHAT DOES IT ALL MEAN?

Once a baby is out of the womb, a midwife or a doctor can often look and say straight away if the baby has a vulva or a penis. The external parts are usually quite obvious, so everyone can see what is there and what isn't there. If there is a penis and testicles, then this baby is called **male**. If there is a vulva, it is quite easy for the parents and doctors to say,

Ah, here is a **FEMALE!**

Sometimes on rare occasions a baby might show **differences in sex development** or **DSD** for short, and it isn't clear which type of genitals they have, or if they have both kinds.

All of this is the **biological sex** of a human baby. Sex is something that humans do (see page 16), but the word also means female or male or intersex. So, if someone asks you what biological sex you are, that is what they mean.

Gender is a bit different and is about how you feel. Your gender can be the same as the sex you are given at birth (for example, someone called 'female' at birth may feel like a 'girl'). But for some people it is different. You might express your gender in what you wear, what you like, what you're called or a hundred different ways. Did you know that when some people talk about gender they use the word *plus* or a + symbol, just like they do when they talk about sexuality? This is to show that there are lots more words for genders and ways to talk about them than the ones we've mentioned here.

So, to sum it up . . .

Your **BIOLOGICAL SEX**
is based on what **genitals** you have.

Your **GENDER** is based on
how you **feel** and often on how you
express yourself.

● **What is the difference between male and female babies?**

All babies have a lot of things that are the same about their bodies when they are born. If you see a baby with its nappy on, it's almost IMPOSSIBLE to tell what its biological sex is. Same little neck, same cute baby arms, same pudgy hands, same mini fingers, same squidgy thighs, same little toes . . . maybe even same brain! We don't really know if there is a male or female brain at birth, but thanks to really clever scientists, we do know that our brains change and grow during our lifetimes.

So, perhaps, **who we are** changes a lot because of things that happen in our life. As we grow up lots of things will have an impact on us – the toys we play with, the clothes we wear and the programmes we watch on TV. We are shaped by how people talk to us, our friends, where we live and the way we are treated at school . . .

So maybe it is **LIFE** that makes us
more *girl-ish* or *boy-ish* or *ourselves-ish*.

● **Lots of the toy babies I've played with don't really look like me. Why not?**

Toys are very important, because they can affect the way you think about the world, and by playing with them you're thinking about different parts of life. Toymakers don't always represent all of the children who play with the toys that they create. Many toy babies and toy dolls in the UK have white skin and often come in pink clothes if they're girls or blue clothes if they're boys, but we know that there are lots of different skin colours and lots of people who don't wear pink or blue or like to wear both.

These toy babies often have a bottle, but we know that there are breastfed babies too! There might not be many toy babies with disabilities, either, even though there are lots of real babies who have disabilities.

It's good to point out when toys **don't** represent the **VARIETY** of people's lives.

It will help adults think about this, and to realize that it's unfair, and that they might be able to get better toys.

● **Can boys have long hair?**

Yes! Of course they can. As bodies change and grow, most people find that their hair grows too – we don't all look like bald babies forever. We get to decide what we do with our own hair. Some people have religious beliefs about their hair. Others have preferences about how they want it to look or feel. Some people think that girls should have long hair and boys should have short hair. Whoever you are, you should be allowed to have whatever hair you believe is right for you!

● **So, if a male has long hair, does that make him a her?**
Nope. Just because you see someone with long hair, that definitely doesn't mean you should say *she* or *her*. Just because someone has a very short and spiky haircut, that doesn't mean you can be sure they're a *he* or a *him*. They might rather be called *they* or *them*! She/her and he/him aren't the words that everyone wants to use any more, and we should all respect that choice.

> Everyone can **CHOOSE** for themselves.
> Whatever their **HAIR**. Whatever their **CLOTHES**.
> Whatever their **BODY**.

If you say the wrong thing by accident, say sorry and try to say it in the right way next time. The important thing is to respect other people's chosen words as much as you can.

● **I heard someone call me a tomboy. What does that mean?**
Tomboy is a very old word from the 1500s used to describe a girl who enjoys activities *traditionally* associated with boys. This means that, in the olden days, some activities were thought of as 'girl things' and others as 'boy things'.

Tomboy is a bit of an annoying word for us. It isn't really very helpful. It is an adult's way of saying, 'Ooooh, that girl isn't doing what girls are SUPPOSED to do.' But we know that girls should be able to do anything they want to do and can be whatever they want to be. There are lots of different ways of being a girl. Maybe that girl is friends with boys or maybe that girl climbs trees or loves riding her bike, and maybe that girl hates wearing dresses, all of which is totally fine. Lots of girls love dresses and lots of girls don't. Some girls like wearing dresses when they are little, but by the time they are a teenager they really, really would **NEVER** wear a dress at all ever again. Some girls refuse to wear dresses for their whole childhood, but suddenly only want to wear skirts. Other girls may just be trouser people all the time and that's just who they are, and that's fine too.

● **My friend is a very *girly* boy. But that's OK, isn't it?**
Yes, of course. There are many different ways to be 'girly'! What does it really mean anyway? There are boys who like wearing dresses or nail varnish. There are boys who like playing with a football or cars. There are boys who like doing both! Sometimes grown-ups find this difficult because they don't realize that it's OK to be a boy and paint your nails if you feel like it. It doesn't mean that you will ALWAYS want to have painted nails. It might just be something you like today, or at this point in your life, or maybe on most days but not all days – or maybe you *will* like it every day for the rest of your life.

YOU CAN BE **ANYONE YOU LIKE** AND YOU CAN **EXPRESS** YOURSELF HOWEVER **YOU** CHOOSE.

Even saying '*girlish*' or '*boyish*' is like putting a **LABEL** on someone, and we don't like labels because humans are more **INTERESTING** than that.

- Is it OK to like princesses AND climbing trees?

- Am I allowed to play football AND paint my nails?

- Is it OK to be a female AND like playing with tools?

The answer to all of these
is a gigantic **YES!** You can do
anything you want.

- **I know someone who calls themselves transgender.
What does that word mean?**

Transgender is a big word that means lots of different things, like a
big umbrella that covers lots of different people's feelings about
themselves. It often means someone who has been called male or
female at birth, but who might feel different from that. People
might want to wear different clothes, or use a different toilet, or
have a different haircut, or might want to change their name. They
might want to tell people that they would like a new word to be
used to describe them, like *she* or *he* or *they*, or all three might feel
right. They might feel uncomfortable about the body parts that
they have, and may have something called **gender dysphoria**,
which is a medical condition and needs a specialist doctor for
medical advice.

The best thing a person can do if they're having confusing
emotions about their body and their feelings is to speak to
someone they trust, like a parent, carer, teacher or doctor. So
transgender doesn't really mean one thing – it means lots of things
to lots of people.

● What if I need to talk to someone about this stuff?

If you want to know more about gender – you might want to chat about clothes, toys or haircuts – or if you feel worried, then think about who your trusted adults are. Look around at the people in your life and think about their biological sex and their gender identity and the choices they have made.

Don't let anyone tell you that you *must* be something, if you don't feel that is what's **INSIDE** you.
JUST BE
YOURSELF!

CHAPTER 5

FAMILY

Relationships are so **IMPORTANT** to our lives, and often the first relationships we build are with our **FAMILY** members.

Whatever shape your family takes, there are lots of things that families do for you, especially when you are little. We need our families to look after us for quite a long time before we can look after ourselves.

In nature it's a bit different. Some animals are born able to do important things straight away. They just come out of the womb able to stand up and eat the same food as their parents. Human babies are a bit helpless when they are born, and can't sit up and feed themselves for ages. Human babies definitely can't stand up until they are almost a whole year old and they can't actually talk until they are about two. So, if a human baby is cold or hot or

sad or hungry or thirsty or needs a new nappy or just wants a snuggle, they can't tell anyone that. They just cry. Human families must do LOADS for their children for a very long time.

As well as making sure you eat and sleep, families are supposed to do other big things like *care for* and *love* and *support* you. They keep you safe and are the ones who try to make sure that nothing bad happens to you. Once you can walk and talk and feed yourself, you still need your family for other important things, like keeping the house warm and cooking healthy food.

These jobs can be done by any family member and are quite often shared because we live in a world where people can make choices about whether they want to be busy at work or busy at home, or both.

Sometimes family members take it in turns, or they swap, or they share the jobs at home and the work jobs. It doesn't matter at all who does what, as long as everyone has the same opportunity . . .

That's the **IMPORTANT** thing.

● **I love my family, but why are they frustrating sometimes?**

The thing about good feelings is that they can sometimes come with bad feelings too, in the same way that light has shadow. We can't pretend that everything is easy-peasy all the time, because it isn't!

So while your family are there to give you security and keep you safe, your family are also there to teach you how to be a good person. Your family will help you learn about the sort of person you want to be. Will you end up being kind? Will you end up being a good listener? Will you end up being a good friend? Can people trust you? Are you good at following instructions? Are you going to be polite? This means that your family are also the people who make the rules. Your family might be the ones who end up telling you off or saying:

NO, don't do **THAT!**

or

Put your socks in the **washing**

or

Put **AWAY** your LEGO

or asking you why your behaviour hasn't been good enough. This might feel REALLY, REALLY ANNOYING, but it is all part of them trying to teach you to be brilliant. They just want you to be a happy child who will turn into a great teenager who will turn into a lovely adult.

Why are siblings so annoying?

Living with someone all the time can be a bit annoying. If you share houses at college or university with your friends, that might be annoying too, especially when they find your chocolate and eat it all or finish the loo roll and you don't realize until it's too late and you are sitting on the loo looking at the empty roll!

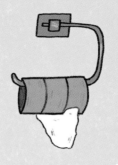

Sharing your space and home and toys with another person is complicated because you're different people with different brains and feelings. Sometimes it can be tricky to put your feelings into words, which means that, if you have a strong feeling and the other person doesn't realize that, it can be tough for them to know how you feel. EVEN if that person is made from the same ingredients as you.

Not AGAIN ...

It doesn't mean it's going to be easy, but learning how to argue and make friends with your siblings will be useful as you get bigger. It might even help you share the next bit of your life with other people.

It's about taking it in **TURNS** and respecting when people need their **OWN SPACE,** and big, **important** things like that.

Even if they do always eat the last biscuit ...

● Do you have to get married to be a family?

Lots of different people believe different things about what grown-ups should do and when they should do it and who they should do it with. Some parents are married and some are not. Some might love not being married forever; some may still get married one day in the future. A marriage doesn't have to be what makes a family.

● Why do people marry?

Marriage is a way of showing the world that you and another adult have found a

MASSIVE GROWN-UP LOVE feeling.

Marriages are planned in different ways depending on culture or religion or belief, but in the UK no one can force you to get married if you don't want to. Usually one person asks the other person. Sometimes they say yes and they might be given a ring, and sometimes they say no.

There are lots of different ways to have a wedding. People who have a religion or a faith might choose to have a religious wedding in a church or a mosque or a synagogue or a temple, so that they can say how much they love each other in front of their God and

their friends who have the same religion. Others choose to have a civil wedding ceremony, and may do this in a non-religious building in a non-religious way.

Some people don't get married, but have a legal ceremony that recognizes them as a couple. This is called a civil partnership. Some couples choose to get married on top of a mountain or on the beach. Some couples have big, massive, noisy parties when they get married. Some couples have quiet weddings and don't invite anyone at all.

● **Can you LOVE someone and not marry them?**
Yes. There are different types of love and it's really important to understand these different types of love.

So let's talk about **love** now.

HOW MANY TYPES OF LOVE CAN YOU THINK OF?

- You can **LOVE** your parents (and they can love you too).
- You can **LOVE** your siblings (even if they are annoying).
- You can **LOVE** your friends (or you might prefer to say you *like* your friends – it's up to you).
- You can **LOVE** your pet (and your pet probably thinks you are great if you feed and stroke it regularly).

- You can **LOVE** your favourite teddy (or your doll or your pencil case).
- You can **LOVE** your pair of pyjamas (but they don't usually love you back).
- You can **LOVE** doing things like gymnastics and swimming (because everyone is allowed to love all sorts of hobbies and activities).

The important thing is knowing that these are all different types of love. We might use the same word, but there are lots of different feelings. And you can really love someone and want to spend the rest of your life with them, but still choose not to get married.

How do you know what romantic LOVE is?

The love you have for a partner or a husband or a wife or a person you choose to spend the rest of your life with is a different feeling from the love you know as a child.

It is **AMAZING** and **MAGICAL** and **wonderful** and **BIG** and SCARY and **powerful** and beautiful and **brilliant** and totally **bamboozling**.

It's the sort of love that is difficult to explain.

A romantic relationship can be a big part of an adult's life, but it isn't everything. Friends, family, work and hobbies are all going to contribute to our lives and can make us really happy in their own right. So a partner can be a great thing to have if you want one, but you need all the other bits too.

I love my best friend. Can we get married?

The simple answer to this is yes, because you probably can. Almost anyone can marry anyone in the UK if they are both over eighteen years old, not closely related, and both want to get married to each other. It's always nice if your families and friends agree too, but that doesn't always happen. It's a big choice, so probably best to wait until you and your best friend are a bit older.

● **Can I marry my parent? I love them and want to live with them forever.**

You can't get married to your parents. It's not allowed in our country (and you aren't allowed to marry your brother or sister or aunties or uncles or grandparents, either).

Lots of children think that, because they love their parents a LOT, they should marry them. Sometimes you might just think that it sounds like a nice idea to live with your parents forever and ever and ever. You can live with them, but you can't marry them.

Sons or daughters do end up living with their adult parents, sometimes caring for them, and that might be what happens to you. You won't know until you get to that bit of your life.

● **Why do some people change their surname when they get married?**

Some people might choose to change their surname when they get married. In the olden days, the male gave the female his name and the female said goodbye to her old name and took on a new one. But you don't have to do that any more. Some people might want to, but plenty might not. Some might want to put their two names together into a double-barrelled surname, or they might share their favourite of the two surnames, or they might make a new name altogether.

What do you think you would do if you had children? And what might they do in turn?

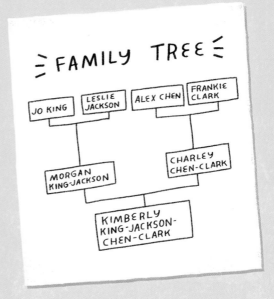

Is marriage forever?

When you choose to get married, you are saying,

I love you **SO** much I want to live with you **FOREVER**.

One of the things that you do when you get married is to promise that you will do your very best to look after each other – even when it's tough – and that, even when you are ill or old, you will try to stay connected to that person forever. BUT sometimes it doesn't work out like that. Sometimes people choose not to be married any more. This is called **separating** or getting **divorced**.

What happens if my parents separate or get divorced?

This may have happened already to you or to one of your friends or family members. Lots of things can change if a relationship ends, but many things can stay the same too. It's up to the adults to decide how this works.

It can mean that people decide they might want to change what they call each other. If they used words like *husband* and *wife*, they might use the words **ex-husband** or **ex-wife**. Sometimes it means that people want to live in different houses. This might be a hard and sad time, but sometimes it's a relief and everyone is very pleased about the change.

Parents might find new partners and start a new life with a different person. If your parent gets married again, then their new partner becomes your **stepmother** or **stepfather**, and if that person has children, then this might mean new **stepbrothers** and **stepsisters** too. If your parent and their new partner have a family, these children are your **half-brother**s and **half-sisters** because they are half the same information as you (as they're made of an egg or sperm from one of your parents). It's important to talk about these **blended** or **patchwork families**, because there isn't just one way of being a family.

● Can adopted people ever find their birth family?

You can have a strong connection with more than one family in your lifetime. Maybe at one stage your adopted family is your strongest sense of belonging. Some adopted people ask to find their birth family, which is sometimes possible. The process involves talking to professionals like a **social worker** or **counsellor**. If finding your birth family is an option, then you might end up forming a really strong connection with them too. Or maybe you can't or don't want to find them. Everyone's story is different.

● How many different types of family are there?

There is **NO** such thing as a *normal* family. Families come in lots of **different** shapes and *sizes* and **combinations**.

★ I have two dads.

★ My auntie has a girlfriend and they are foster parents.

★ I only know my mum.

★ We used to be three children, but my sibling died, so now we are two children.

★ My grandparents are the people I live with.

★ My dad died before I was born, but I have an amazing stepfather.

★ I don't live with my parent. I live in a care home with other kids like me.

- ⭐ My parent isn't a *he* or a *she*, and has chosen to use the pronouns *they* and *them*.

- ⭐ I have loads of half-siblings and step-siblings.

- ⭐ My mum used to be married to my dad, but now she has a girlfriend.

- ⭐ My dad was called *female* at birth, but he is transgender and he is a *man*.

- ⭐ My mum and dad aren't married.

- ⭐ My family lives with lots of other families travelling around the place.

- ⭐ I'm an only child, with no brothers or sisters.

- ⭐ My parents live in different houses, but they are good friends.

- ⭐ My dad will be in prison for a long time, so we go and visit him.

- ⭐ Me and my parents live here, but the rest of our family lives in another country.

- ⭐ I am adopted, but my family are still my family.

- ⭐ I go to a boarding school so, during term time, the adults who work there look after me.

CHAPTER 6

CONSENT
AND
RESPECTING
OTHERS

Understanding the needs of **others** in relationships is **REALLY** important. This chapter is about something called **consent**.

We talk about consent a lot. It is VERY important. You are practising consent all the time, but you might not even know it.

You might know about consent from school, where a parent or caregiver must give their consent for you to go on a school trip. They usually have to sign a form and give permission for the teachers to put you on a bus and take you to a museum or a swimming pool or a science centre.

But consent in relationships is about more than permission. It's not about one person asking and the other signing a form saying 'yes' or 'no'.

It's about *equality, agreement* and *communication*. You can't just pick up someone's water bottle or put on their hoodie or help yourself to their phone if they haven't given you their consent. That wouldn't be OK.

Let's think about high-fives. How do you know if someone wants to do a high-five with you? Do you just assume that everyone likes high-fives and go straight on in there with an open palm and swipe them hard? How can you tell if someone doesn't want to do high-fives with you?

WORDS

You could ask them, 'Hey, do you want to do a high-five with me?' They may say yes. They may say no. They may say, 'Errrrrm . . .' But they may not feel confident enough to say no. They may just go along with it, even though they didn't really agree. They might not want to leave you hanging. It's a weird feeling being left hanging, but does that mean someone should just go along with the high-five anyway? Even if they don't feel comfortable? What does 'Errrrrm . . .' mean? It certainly doesn't mean yes.

We can't always rely on words, but there are other ways that a person might signal how they feel.

BODY LANGUAGE

Body language is useful too. If a person puts their hands in their pockets or crosses their arms . . . maybe they don't want to do the high-five.

The reality is that not everyone is a high-five kind of person. Some will, some won't, some do, some don't. There are a few folks who might be fist-bump people. Or they might have sweaty hands just now. Or they might want to keep their hands to themselves. And it *is* a choice. A really important choice. Everyone needs to have a voice in this sort of choice.

It's not always easy to listen to other people, to work out what they are feeling or to take it in turns, but these are really important things to understand if you want to have happy relationships.

How can I tell people NO?

There are so many different ways to say NO! If you use your body you can:

- **CROSS** your arms

- Put your **HANDS** in your pockets

- Frown, scowl and have an **ANNOYED FACE**

- Turn **AWAY**

- Make yourself big and strong and **POWERFUL** and look them in the eye

- Walk **AWAY** and go somewhere else

- Pretend you need a wee and go to the toilet and **SHUT THE DOOR.**

If you use your words you can say:

Please **STOP**

I am **not** enjoying this

This **isn't** fun for me

No, **don't do that**

I don't like it when
you do that to me

Or (if it's not working very well with your words) you can go and
ask a grown-up to help you, because there is usually a teacher or a
parent around and they will be able to help you say **NO!**

What about my online friends? Does consent matter with them too?

YES. Consent is just as important online as it is offline, and it needs rules too. The people you are friends with online might be people you know or people you think you know or total strangers. They can be nice to you and they can be mean to you, just like people you talk to face-to-face. They should never make you feel like you have to do something you don't want to do. You always have a voice and a choice, and if you are worried, tell a trusted adult.

How do I say NO online?

If people ask you for personal information like your name or address or phone number, or ask you to do something that makes you feel uncomfortable, or if you just don't like the situation, you can say no in lots of different ways.

No thanks. This doesn't feel right.

Nope – I don't know who you are.

I wouldn't say that to a real person offline, so I shouldn't say it online.

I don't give photos to people I don't know in a shop, so I'm not going to give you a photo!

I don't share my address or phone number with strangers on the street, so why would I give it to you?

But we don't know each other in real life, so I'm gonna say no to that offer!

My parents have told me not to share online.

There is an adult in the room with me and they don't think this is a good idea.

My teacher told me not to, so I am going to say no thanks!

If you are uncomfortable online, or you have seen something on the internet that you are worried about, you can always **exit** the chat, **leave** the group and **log off**. You should always let a trusted adult know what is going on, and they can help you say no.

● Sometimes my parents take photos and I don't want them to. Then they SHARE them without asking. It's so annoying.

You are **100** per cent allowed to say **NO** to grown-ups if it is something you feel **strongly** about.

You can use all the body-language ways and word ways of saying no. You can go into a bit more detail and explain why you don't want that photo taken, then ask the grown-up nicely NOT to share it online. If you wanted to, you might be able to choose the photo that they share, or draw a picture of yourself instead. You could say,

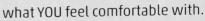

Please could you ask **me** first?

Or you could just say no. Parents are usually just proud of you at sports day or on your first day of school or at your birthday and want to share this with family and friends, **BUT IT IS STILL YOUR CHOICE.** If you don't like the feeling of something, then you can always say **NO THANKS!**

● Help! I hate having to kiss my granny when I don't want to!

There are lots of ways of showing people that we like or love them. Kissing and hugging is just one of these ways. Sometimes we want to show someone we love them by squeezing them really tight and smothering them in kisses, but at other times that is the last thing we want! It's really important to know what YOU feel comfortable with. There are other ways to show love for each other, like helping someone, listening to them or making a card for them. If you do not want to be cuddled, you are always allowed to say or show that, and then the other person will know that you don't want a cuddle any more and should respect that and stop.

● **I don't like tickles, cuddles and squeezes with everyone.**

Different people like being touched in different ways and not all body parts feel the same. Cheeks feel different from ears and hands and feet and your chest or buttocks or eyes. Strokes, rubs, pinches, tickles and scratches feel COMPLETELY different.

Certain people are allowed to do certain touches. It might be nice for your mum to stroke your back before you go to bed, but it might feel weird if a friend did it.

You get to make your
own rules about
YOUR BODY

but it's tricky when some people have different rules from you.

The important thing is that you know that you never have to do something that you don't like doing. You should never hurt anyone or let anyone hurt you. You need to respect each other's rules, especially when it comes to bodies and being naked.

● **Being naked is confusing. Sometimes people say it's OK and sometimes people say it's not.**

Even when we are dressed, some parts might be naked all the time, like faces, hands and sometimes legs or arms. In some situations we might be a little bit naked, like in swimming pools or at gymnastics or at ballet. We could be half naked for a short amount of time, like when we go to the toilet. Sometimes we are really, completely and utterly naked, like when we are in the bath or the shower.

Different people will have different FEELINGS about being naked.

Some people are very comfortable without their clothes on and may walk around the house or even go to special beaches where everyone has agreed to wear no clothes. Other people will feel like they want to be covered up all the time, which might be because their religion or faith tells them this and they respect these rules. So if your family and religion tell you that bodies should be covered up and private and you shouldn't show skin, then that is your story, but it might not be everyone's story.

● Should I lock the door for privacy when I go to the toilet in the supermarket?

How we behave at home is different from how we behave when we are out in public, for example when we are at the supermarket.

Some people go to the toilet with a grown-up if they need help unzipping zips, undoing buttons that are really tricky or wiping. Others like to shut the door and be more independent and peaceful. When we are out in public, it's sometimes tricky because we don't know who else might come into the toilets, and other people don't want to walk in and find you sitting there with your pants round your ankles. The problem is that locking the door might be scary for you or make your parent worry, so you could ask

someone you trust to stand by the door to keep strangers away. Or maybe you're OK on your own!

As we grow older, we can begin to feel like these parts are more private, so it makes total sense to ask for privacy for your private moments.

Which parts are private?

Think about being at a swimming pool. People tend to cover up the bits they think are private, but if you really look around you'll see that there are lots of different people who think lots of different things. Some people wear little Speedos while others prefer big, baggy board shorts, or tiny bikinis, or sporty swimming costumes, or shorts and T-shirts, or burkinis that cover their whole body.

Every person can form their own idea of private. The thing that most people agree on is that what's covered by your pants is DEFINITELY private for everyone, which is why we don't see people without their pants on in the local swimming pool or at school or at the supermarket – or anywhere else for that matter!

Even if pants are private, I like being naked . . . Is that OK?

There are rules, and these rules are about behaving differently in different places. Of course, it is OK to be naked in the right place with the right people at the right time.

Being **happy** with your body and
seeing it and knowing it and loving it is a big
part of being **HUMAN**.

It's your body, so it is a very good thing to love it. Whatever shape it is, whatever it looks like, it is your body and there is nothing wrong with being naked. But make sure you think about the rules. The rules are usually about the other people around you. Make sure you think carefully about those people. Do they need to see you naked? Are they trusted adults? Will seeing you naked make them feel uncomfortable?

IF YOU ARE **UNSURE**, YOU CAN ALWAYS ASK A **PARENT** OR **CAREGIVER** WHAT THEY THINK, AND THEY CAN HELP YOU MAKE A **GOOD** DECISION.

Is it OK for me to touch myself?

Some people do things with their own body - suck their thumb, twiddle their hair, pick their nose, tickle or stroke themselves. Children and adults get to choose what they want to do to their own bodies, but as we get older, we must think about the other people around us.

Some things are **public**
(for everyone) and some things are
PRIVATE (just for you).

Laughing, sneezing and coughing are *public* things. We all do them and we don't mind if other people around us do them. Burping or farting might be considered a *private* thing. When you get old enough to know that burps and farts aren't polite and don't make everyone around you feel good, then you learn to control them and hold them in and do them in a more private place.

Picking your nose is a **BIG ONE** . . . It might make other people feel yukky, but that doesn't mean it is bad or wrong. It just means that you shouldn't really pick your nose in a lesson or at the table when everyone is eating. It is more appropriate to go and pick your nose in the bathroom with a tissue.

It's similar with your penis or your vulva. Putting your hand in your pants to touch your own penis or vulva isn't wrong, but it might make other people feel uncomfortable. It's not strange or dirty, but it is something that is best done in private. You need to be private with it, care for it and keep it healthy. Just make sure you are gentle and that it feels nice.

When is it OK to let someone touch my penis or vulva?

There are rules about other people looking at or touching your genitals. Sometimes it is OK to let trusted adults look at or touch your penis or testicles or vulva or vagina or anus for a good reason like your health or if they need to help you wash.

Your parents are usually the ones who you trust, so most of the time it is OK to talk to them about your genitals and most of the time it is OK to show them ALL your body parts. They did a lot of this when you were a baby and needed your nappy changed. They did a lot of washing when you were a toddler in the bath.

Doctors and nurses should also be trusted people and it's important to ask them for help if there is a problem with a body part. If your vulva or penis has an itch or a rash or hurts, then they might need to examine it, but your parent will be there too. Even though you might feel a bit awkward about your genitals, you should feel safe around these professionals because they are there to help you.

Who should I tell if I am worried?

If you are ever worried that a friend or an adult or someone else has shared something, or tickled or squeezed or cuddled or touched you in a way you don't like, or if you've seen something on the internet that you're worried about, then you must ask for help. You should always say no if you don't want someone to touch you, and no one is allowed to touch or change a part of your body without your consent. You need to find trusted adults, like a parent or doctor or nurse or teacher, and tell them if there is something you don't feel OK with.

Who are **your** trusted adults? Who would you tell?

CHAPTER 7

FEELINGS

FEELINGS is a word that can mean different **things** at different **times**.

Think about feeling objects. The difference between feeling a stone or a feather. Feeling a wet thing or a dry thing. Feeling something smooth or something spiky. These are outside feelings related to **touch**.

OUCH

Feelings aren't always related to touch. The word *feelings* can also be used to talk about how you feel inside.

You might have heard people talking about having *feelings for someone*. This means that they feel a powerful feeling about this person. Maybe they have a crush on them. Maybe they really, really like them. They might LOVE them a little bit.

How do you know that you have feelings for someone? It is different for everyone, but it usually makes you feel ALL FUNNY! Some people say it makes them feel a bit giggly, or maybe even a bit embarrassed for no particular reason. It might feel like there are butterflies in your tummy, a magnetic pull between you or a warm fuzzy feeling.

There are also a huge range of INSIDE FEELINGS called **EMOTIONS** that can leave you feeling good or bad.

These inside feelings are much more complicated than outside ones, because you can't see them or touch them and the words for them aren't as easy to understand.

Any different combination of these emotions can mean we end up feeling good or feeling bad.

HAPPY

QUIET

BORED

SAD

SCARED

ANGRY

WORRIED

ANXIOUS

CALM

KIND

GRUMPY

DISAPPOINTED

SAFE

LOVED

JEALOUS

EXCITED

CONFIDENT

SHY

It's great to know the words for these feelings, partly because it helps you explain them to other people. It is really useful to work out what has made the feeling inside you. It's great if you can think about other people's feelings too.

It's good to know which feelings you like. It's also important to recognize that sometimes we all have feelings we don't like. Our emotions will sometimes overwhelm us, and we may feel

REALLY **CROSS** or ANGRY or **shouty** or sulky.

At moments like this we need to try to remember the words for these feelings, talk about them to someone else, find out where the feeling has come from, and choose the best way to behave (even if that's really hard because it's difficult to make good choices when we are full of big emotions).

It's good to know what makes you feel better too. If you like cuddles. If you like duvets and snuggly blankets. If you like hot baths or cool showers. If you can do things that soothe you – like stroking a pet or swishing the glitter in a snow globe – to help your emotions settle and reduce any panicky feelings.

It's important to recognize if you don't like things too. If you don't like being the centre of attention. If you don't like having your photograph taken. If you don't like people squishing and squashing and wrestling with you. If you don't like loud noises. If you don't like the dark. That's all OK too.

You are **allowed** to say which feelings you **LIKE** and which feelings you **don't like**. The more you use your words and tell people about your feelings, the more they can look after **YOUR NEEDS**.

● **How can I make myself feel happier when I feel sad or cross or worried?**

There are all sorts of ways you can do this. You could:

- use your words to explain the feeling

- not keep secrets

- talk to people around you about where that feeling came from

- ask for help

- sleep well

- eat well

- drink water

- ask for details about things that are going to happen (because sometimes surprises are stressful)

- get some fresh air and go for a run or a bike ride

- do something you love

- find **mindful** moments by breathing slowly and deeply, or by counting to ten in your head

- write it down

- get lost in a book

- think about other people and do a kind thing for someone else (because kindness often makes us feel better).

● What should I do if I notice a big change in my friend's feelings?

Friends are really important and we need to look after them. As you get bigger and spend more time with your friends, it becomes even more important to keep a close eye on them.

Sometimes friends go a bit quiet, or a bit sad, or a bit cross, or are not their usual self. If you know what they are like on a good day and you can see that something isn't quite right, that's a feeling you need to listen to. You could ask them if they want to talk. If you're still worried, being brave and telling a trusted adult – maybe their parent, maybe a teacher, maybe your parent – is the best thing you can do. It might not be anything to worry about – they may just be very busy and tired or a bit ill or fighting off a cold or a bug – but there may be something more serious happening, so it is always good to step up, step in and ask for help!

HOW ARE YOU FEELING?

● I've heard the words *mental health* – what do they mean?

Mental means linked to the **mind** and **HEALTH** is related to **wellbeing**.

We all have **mental health** because we all have a mind. Sometimes people's minds can feel easy to make sense of. Sometimes people's minds can feel more complicated.

So mental health is the wellbeing of your mind – it's a bit about feelings and emotions, but more about how you think and your moods. A person's mental health might not be obvious to others because you can't see it immediately, like you can see a bruise or a broken arm. But in the same way that you know without seeing it if you have a toothache or a sore stomach, you might be aware of your own mental health. Sometimes you can feel it, and even though it might be really hard, you can try to communicate it to people around you by telling them about it.

We all have different heads, different brains and different thoughts. Problems can arise if our thoughts get in a pickle because it's hard to understand them. Thinking and moods can change how we see the world and sometimes this can be overwhelming.

When it is **overwhelming**, the best thing to do
is to tell a trusted **ADULT.**

You could say:

Can I talk to you, please?
I need **HELP**
because I am having a
tough time …

You could draw a **picture** or tell a **STORY** if that makes it easier to **explain** your feelings.

It's really important to look after the health of your mind just like you would look after the health of your body. So, just as with your body, telling a trusted adult or teacher is the best way to look after your mental health, because they can usually help you get better.

CHAPTER 8
FRIENDS

Friends can be the **best** people ever. They are there to have fun with, to play with, to **SUPPORT** you, and to talk to you about important, **challenging** and SILLY things.

You might have lots of friends, or maybe just one or two really special ones. Your friends might be people who live in the same house as you, people at school, or people you do hobbies with at the weekend. They may live close to you or might live miles and miles away and connect with you online. You may play games, chat or just like being in the same room as them without having to say very much at all!

Friends teach us things about ourselves and friendships are very important relationships.

Respecting each other is one of the most important ingredients of a friendship. Knowing what your friends like and don't like can sometimes be tough. You might think that your friend is enjoying a game you are playing, a film that you are watching or a meal that you are eating together, but actually they might be having a horrid time. How do we know that our friends are happy and enjoying the same things as us? We can tell from their smiles, their giggles, or they might be making happy noises, or they might be using their words.

Sometimes, though, a friend might tell you with words that they are LOVING this film or REALLY enjoying this game, but they might not know exactly how they feel or might even be pretending and actually having a rubbish time! Sometimes they may be a bit quiet, and this might be because they aren't enjoying themselves, but haven't been able to tell anyone yet. Maybe they are scared they might let you down, or they might need a little bit of help to feel brave enough to say how they really feel.

You could choose a special code word you can each use when you feel that something isn't working out for you. If you are wrestling with your friend and rolling around in a rough-and-tumble sort of way, how do you know when they want to stop? They could shout out

STOP! **HELP!** **ENOUGH!**

or a code word like

BANANAS!

which actually means

This **isn't** fun for me any more!

It might sound strange, but some siblings and friends prefer an agreed code word because it means that you are serious. It can be tough being a good friend because humans aren't the best at reading minds. Accepting that other people like different things and behave in different ways isn't easy for everyone, but trying your best to think about how your friends feel is part of being a really good friend.

What should I do if I fall out with my best friend?

It's great to have a best friend, but it can be tough too. Friendships are complicated and don't always last forever. A best friend can change, and you can form new connections with different people. This isn't always easy, but friendship is how we learn about ourselves and about each other. You don't have to have a best friend if you don't want one – you might be more of a big-group-of-friends person.

The only thing we can really say about FRIENDS is that you need to **make sure** that everyone involved is happy being in that friendship – that you are all **COMFORTABLE** with each other, and that you all feel safe and secure. That you are **happy** to be friends, but also happy to have **other** friends. That you are **EQUAL** and take it in turns.

One friend shouldn't be more powerful than the other friend, and if a friendship starts to feel wonky, there is a problem. If a friend is making you do stuff you don't want to do, or they are not letting you be friends with other people, then you must TELL SOMEONE straight away, like a trusted adult.

It's horrid feeling left out. What if I can see that someone feels a bit sad or lonely?

Being left out of a game or not being invited to a party is difficult. People can feel left out for lots of reasons. They might feel sad or lonely because others are being mean, or because their life is tricky just now. You can't always tell when someone's struggling, but sometimes people might be sad or cross when they're having a hard time. There are so many reasons to feel like the odd one out, or like you are on your own, or that no one understands what it is like to be you.

Unfortunately, we can't just wave a magic wand and make it all better, but we can tell you that you aren't the first person or the last person to feel like that. If you are brave enough to tell someone, they will probably be able to help you. It might be that a chat or a hug or a visit to a counsellor can make it easier.

If the lonely person can't tell anyone, not even a sibling or a cousin or someone in class, and you can see that they aren't quite right, then you should step in and see if you can find a trusted adult to help that person with their feelings and show them that they aren't alone.

What about bullies?

Bullying is **NEVER** ok.

It means that one person or a group of people are hurting your feelings or your body, and they might be doing this again and again and again. This means that the power in the relationship is wonky – the bully thinks they have control over decisions and they get to choose what happens to you. Even if the person is much older than you, or seems like they have more friends than you, it is still very wrong and they are a bully. Bullying can happen face-to-face or online. Whether it is someone at school, at home or online, the same rules apply.

- If something doesn't feel right, you don't have to be involved in it.

- If you feel uncomfortable, you can walk away or close down that chat.

- If you feel scared, that isn't OK.

- If you feel like you don't have any power, the friendship isn't equal.

- You must ask for help (even if you're not sure).

- Remember, it's not your fault.

- Being mean back doesn't help, so don't reply with bad words or rude comments.

- Try saying:

I **DON'T** like it when you say/do that.

or

Please stop. I'm going to go now.

- Be kind to yourself by hanging out with someone who makes you feel great!

- Put yourself around people where the power is equal.

- And remember that sometimes the bully needs help too.

CHAPTER 9

WHAT HAPPENS NEXT?

We've spoken about lots of things that have already happened to you, and might be happening to you now, but you might also have started to think about what comes next. So let's talk about growing up.

You have changed **so much** since being a baby. You have done **LOADS** of growing, getting **bigger** and **stronger**.

You turned from a baby into a toddler, and you've learned new things, which might include eating and talking and walking.

You have turned from a toddler into a child. You're probably attending school and have learned even more new skills, like literacy and numeracy. You may eat more varieties of food and you might even eat a lot of it ALL THE TIME. You might have been aware of things changing with your body, like losing some of your baby teeth or getting bigger feet.

Over the next few years your body and mind will continue to grow and change. The stage of growth between being a child and an adult is called **adolescence** and all **adolescents** will go through a set of changes. This is what we call **puberty**.

Puberty happens when new hormones start telling the body to behave in a slightly different way.

The brain releases a new set of messages, and tells all the other bits of the body to change what they are doing.

This might start off with a few small outside changes that happen gradually, like:

★ getting a lot taller

★ getting wider hips or broader shoulders

★ possibly some voice changes

★ getting a bit hairier

★ being a bit sweaty and making new smells

★ maybe even getting greasier hair

★ having oilier skin and perhaps becoming a bit spotty.

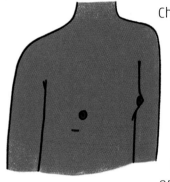

Chests and nipples can start to change. This can happen to everyone. It usually begins with the nipple area getting a bit puffy and looking a bit different (sometimes like there is a pea under the skin). In most male bodies, these swollen nipples tend to settle down and not develop any further. In most female bodies, they carry on growing and may turn into a pair of grown-up breasts, boobs, boobies or whatever you want to call them.

There will also be some changes inside that start going on behind the scenes. These changes are all about the eggs and sperm. Going through puberty means moving towards having an adult body so that one day you may be able to reproduce and create children of your own (if you want to).

During female puberty, the vulva may change shape and size, and there is likely to be some **pubic hair** that grows around the outside, and it might start to feel a bit different too. You might notice that it releases a small amount of white or clear fluid called **vaginal discharge**. This might have always been there, or maybe it's new to you – but it's very natural and healthy. The internal female genitals keep themselves clean. You can keep the external vulva clean by regularly washing with water.

Before puberty, the ovaries don't do very much, but once your body begins to change they start releasing eggs. There are thousands of eggs in your ovaries and at some point during puberty your body starts **ovulating**. This is when an egg is released from the ovaries and travels down the fallopian tube. Most people only release one egg during each ovulation.

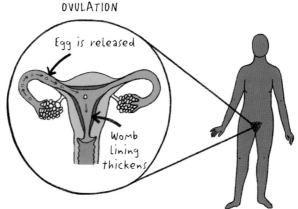

OVULATION

Egg is released

Womb
Lining
thickens

The womb also starts behaving differently. When an egg is released, the womb gets ready for a baby (just in case the egg meets a sperm). This means that the womb creates a soft and comfortable lining. But most of the time there is no sperm. So no baby. And the cosy, comfy womb lining isn't required, so it comes out of the vagina. This is menstrual blood, which some people call a **period** or **menstruation**.

Periods are very different for **EVERYONE**.

Did you know that some people get **cramps** in their womb and feel a bit groggy and tired when they are menstruating? It can be helpful to use a hot-water bottle, have a long bath, drink plenty of water, exercise and get more rest. There are lots of different ways to look after yourself during this time, and you can work out what is best for you.

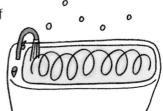

Periods might happen when you're younger, at the age of eight or nine, but mostly they start a bit later, after the age of eleven. It's also fine not to get periods until much later, up to around the age of sixteen. There are lots of people who can help you understand how periods work and help you take care of yourself during your period in a way that is right for you.

During male puberty, which may start at about the age of eleven or any time up to the age of sixteen, the penis might get bigger and might sometimes go stiffer more often, which is called an erection. Washing your penis regularly, including around the foreskin area, will help keep it healthy. Usually there will be some new pubic hair growing around the testicles and scrotum area.

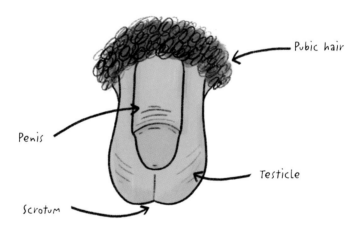

Pubic hair

Penis

Testicle

Scrotum

Before puberty, the testicles don't do very much, but once your body starts maturing the testicles may change shape and start a very important job. They start making sperm that travel in a creamy white fluid called semen. Sometimes a small amount of semen can come out of the tip of the penis. This could happen at any point, but if this happens when you are asleep it is called a **nocturnal emission** or a **wet dream**. If this happens to you, it's very healthy and you don't need to worry – you can keep yourself clean by changing your bedding and having a wash.

Everyone experiences puberty differently, but the important things to remember are:

- You don't know WHEN these things will happen to you. You might be eight, eleven, thirteen or even eighteen.

- You don't know what order things will happen in.

- It will happen to pretty much everyone at some point, so don't panic if you are the first one or the last one. It's not a race!

- It won't hurt and it's not bad. It's very healthy, natural and to be expected.

- You can always ask a trusted adult if you want to know more. They've all been through puberty so will be able to tell you about how it felt for them. But you shouldn't compare yourself to anyone. Your puberty will be yours and it will be unique, just like you are.

My friends' bodies are different from mine. Why?
Some things about our bodies are similar and some things about our bodies are different. If you look at everyone in your class at school, some people might have curly hair. Some might have very, very straight hair. Everyone has a different skin colour. Some people have freckles. Some people have disabilities. Some people have bigger or smaller feet.

When we talked about the human life cycle, we talked about the fact that you are a combination of the bits of you that came from the sperm and the bits that came from the egg. So if that sperm and egg have made you a little bit shorter than your friends, or a little bit taller than you want to be, you can't change that! We know it can be annoying . . . but it is YOU!

WHEN YOU REACH PUBERTY, PEOPLE'S BODIES WILL CHANGE AT DIFFERENT RATES.

Remember what it was like when you started losing your baby teeth? Everyone's teeth fall out at different ages. It can be hard if you're waiting and wishing to lose your teeth, but everything happens in a different order for each of us. Puberty is similar in this way – everyone has an experience that's personal to them.

We are all **different** and come in various shapes, **SIZES** and **colours** because we are all made of **different** combinations of sperm and eggs. We're **UNIQUE**, and that's just how it is.

● **My parent has a deep voice. Will mine change too?**
When bodies go through puberty, one of the big changes is that the person's voice starts to sound a bit different. Not everyone knows that female voices change a little, but most people know that male voices change quite a lot – they get lower and deeper. Scientists still aren't really sure why this happens, but if we look at animals, we might find the answer. Male animals quite often have a different voice when they grow older, and we think this is to attract a mate (someone to have a family with) and maybe to scare away competition (so that no one comes near to their family or hurts them).

In humans, the hormone called **testosterone** tells the **voice box** (or Adam's apple) to get bigger, and the stretchy bits of cartilage (called **vocal cords**) inside the throat change shape, getting longer and thicker, and therefore make a different sound. It's a bit like twanging an elastic band. If you twang a little elastic band, it sounds very high and produces a gentle noise like a *ping*. This is very different from twanging a big old piece of rubber, which would be lower and slower and sound more like a *doi-oi-oing*.

Will I get more hair?

Hair changes so much during our lives. Baby hair is thin and soft and wispy. Children's hair can be a totally different colour from baby hair, and then it changes again when you go through puberty, and can be darker or thicker or there can be more of it. And that's before we even start talking about what happens to hair when you get old!

The hair on our bodies changes too. Some bodies can grow hair that's much thicker and darker than others can grow. Some people can get thicker eyebrows, or a hairy chest, or a hairy back and shoulders or legs. You can start to grow hair on your face – usually only on your chin and neck. Hair can grow under your arms (most bodies going through puberty will experience this).

Someone might grow a little bit of hair. Another person might grow a LOT.

And there is also pubic hair which grows around the penis and vulva area. It doesn't grow ON the penis, but around the scrotum and testicles at the base of the penis. And it doesn't grow INSIDE the vagina, but around the outer labia of the vulva. This hair is sometimes dark (but can come in different colours) and it is often a bit thicker and sometimes curly. It is really useful because it is there to cushion and protect your delicate genitals, a bit like padding in a parcel or wearing protective puffy clothes to keep your body safe.

Why do some people take their body hair off?

You don't have to do anything to your body if you don't want to. These are all choices. Yes, some people might choose to have the hair on their heads cut at the hairdresser, and some people might choose to shave off their beards, or might choose to tidy up their eyebrow hair, or shave or wax or tweezer or epilate or thread or laser other hairs on their body. The choices you make about YOUR body are YOUR choices to make.

You should **only** ever remove hair if you are doing it for the **RIGHT REASONS** and know all of the options available to make an **informed** choice.

Some people might . . .

- be really proud of their hairy bits
- be really content with body hair and keep all of it
- just keep a little bit of hair here and there
- have a belief or a religion that tells them certain things about their body hair and what to do with it
- want to have no hair in some places.

There are so many options available when it comes to your body hair, and talking about it with your trusted adults will help you make the right decision for you.

Will I need to wear a bra one day? How will I know?

Bras are funny. You might have seen one before or you might not. You can wear them like goggles or headphones . . . But, really, they are for breasts. There are lots of types of bras to choose from – bralettes, sports bras, bras with and without underwire, crop tops and padded bras. Some people love them. Some people hate them. Some people wear one every day. Some people never wear one. They come in lots of different shapes and sizes and colours and patterns, so there is a lot of choosing to do to find the right bra for you, because everyone's breasts are different.

How do I choose a bra if I want to wear one?

When the time comes, it's best to go to a professional. Lots of shops offer a free measuring service, where a friendly and experienced bra fitter will help you choose the right size so that you can get underwear that really fits and is good for your body.

Bad underwear is **rubbish**.
It doesn't feel good or look good and, if it doesn't fit properly, then it's **NOT** healthy for your growing body to keep growing in!

Will I need to use any new things when I reach puberty? I don't know when I should start using deodorant . . .

Besides growing hair, the other thing that happens in your underarm area during puberty is sweat. Armpits make more sweat if you do lots of exercise, if you get stressed or worried, or if you are just living in a very, very hot place with toasty warm sunshine and lovely blue skies. Sweat is great and helps cool you down.

Did you know that **scientists** think the reason we have eyebrows is to stop **sweat** from going into our eyes?

The sweat that happens under our arms is a bit different from other sweat because it can be a bit stinky. It has a certain pong to it. Some people call this smell **body odour** or **BO**. It's nothing to worry about. When people are going through puberty, sometimes they need to have a few more showers than usual. You might want to invest in some products from the shop, but don't feel that you NEED to go and buy a squillion things from your local pharmacy. Sometimes these sorts of products are bad for your body and bad for the environment. Companies are trying to make money and sometimes they try to sell stuff to young people who are worried. You can, of course, go and buy a few bits and bobs, but it's really important to realize that some products contain chemicals and can have an impact on the environment. You can make the right choice for you.

You might use . . .

- deodorant or antiperspirant to help with sweat and body odour – this could be a roll-on, an aerosol, a stick or even something more natural, like a crystal or a saltwater spray

- gentle soap or cleansing gel to keep your body and face clean

- moisturizer to help with dry skin.

If you have any questions about the skin on your body or face, you can talk to a trusted adult. Doctors and nurses will be able to give you advice if you have any serious skin concerns.

● **What choices can I make about the environment?**
Everything we buy for our bodies has an impact on the planet.
Think about a nice-looking shampoo or conditioner you might
want to buy.

What **factory** was it made in? Which **COUNTRY**
was it made in? How was it **transported** here? What
INGREDIENTS are in it? How much **plastic** is in the bottle?
Is it a **single-use** plastic? Are you going to throw the
bottle away? Are you going to **refill** the bottle?

Or think about an aerosol of deodorant.

What **GAS** is in there to make it spray? Is it
good for the **ENVIRONMENT?** Is it good for
your skin? Can you **recycle** that packaging
where you live? Will it end up in **landfill?**

These are all questions that you can think about when you buy and
use up products so that you can make an informed decision about
what to get.

● **Do I get to use all the period stuff that's at home in
the cupboard under the sink?**
It's normal to be aware of the period stuff in the bathroom. Or in a
handbag. Or in the restaurant toilet in a little basket. Or in a
machine in the ladies' loos in supermarkets. They might sometimes
look like sweets or air fresheners, but they are actually used to help
with periods. If you have ovaries with eggs in them, and a womb

and a vagina, then it is likely that one day you will get a period, but even if you are a person with a penis it is still very useful for you to understand periods. You will know someone who gets periods, so it's really important to know about them so that you can be caring and understanding if someone tells you about how they are feeling.

About once a month a bit of blood is released from the womb. People have a choice of products they can buy to absorb and catch the blood so it doesn't go on their clothes. This way, the blood ends up in the toilet or in the sink or in the bin and not on pants or clothes or bedding.

There are lots of options for dealing with period blood, but until you have started your periods you don't need to panic. You can ask the trusted adults around you who have periods about what they do, and they will explain these options to you.

Let's look at some of the options . . .

Panty liners

Panty liners are a small bit of disposable padding that you can stick on the inside of your pants. They only catch a little bit of blood, which means that they might be good for the start or end of your period, or if you only have very light periods.

You should change your panty liners regularly – probably every few hours, or when they are full. You remove them from your pants and put them in the **sanitary bin** afterwards. They can only be used once.

Disposable pads

A pad looks like a panty liner with padding and a plastic under layer, but is thicker and more absorbent. They come in different shapes and sizes, which are suitable for different people depending on their **flow** – this means how heavy a person's period is, and it can vary a lot. Disposable pads stick on to your pants and can have wings that wrap round the sides of the underwear. They soak up blood and need to be changed every few hours. They can be only used once – when you have finished with them, you can throw them in the sanitary bin.

Washable pads

These are similar to disposable pads, but they are made of soft fabric so you can wash them, like your clothes, and use them again. They might have poppers to help make them even more secure. They are better for the environment.

Period underwear

Period underwear means special pants made specifically for catching blood. They are tight and comfortable, and they have a waterproof lining and inbuilt padding to absorb the period blood. They can be washed and used again, which means that they are an environmentally friendly choice.

Tampons

Tampons are like compact bits of cotton wool, about the size of your little finger, with a shortish length of soft string attached to one end. They come in different shapes and sizes, which have different levels of absorbency (this means how much blood they can absorb). They go inside the vagina so that all the blood is absorbed before it comes out.

Some tampons have an applicator that is made out of cardboard, single-use plastic or reusable materials, and can make it easier to put the tampon in. You insert the applicator into the vagina, then push it up gently to release the tampon from the applicator into the vaginal entrance, leaving the soft string outside the body. There are always clear instructions to help you with this. Some tampons don't have an applicator, so you can insert them into the vagina using your finger, pushing it up to a place that feels comfortable.

A tampon can only stay in the body for 4–8 hours and then it needs to be removed, using the soft string, and thrown away in a sanitary bin. Then a new tampon can be inserted.

Tampons can be particularly useful if you're doing something like swimming, where you aren't able to wear a pad .

Menstrual cups

Menstrual cups go inside you, like a tampon, but are made of silicone and shaped like a cup. They sit inside the vaginal entrance, and collect any menstrual blood.

To insert a menstrual cup, you fold it and push it into the vagina. The cup has a silicone stem, which helps to pull it out once it is full. You can't feel it once it is inside and it just needs to be emptied when it is full – at least once a day – to be rinsed. This is simple in a cubicle with a sink or at home. Menstrual cups are slightly more expensive than other period care products at first, but can last for up to ten years, which actually makes them very affordable. They are reusable so are a good choice for the environment and, like tampons, are great for swimming and other physical activities like yoga or gymnastics.

Until it's **your turn** you won't know what the right option for **you** is!

THIS DECISION IS ABOUT YOUR BODY, HOW MUCH THINGS COST, WHAT WORKS FOR YOU, AND THE ENVIRONMENT TOO ...

It's hard to be really prepared all of the time, so if you're in a muddle with your period and don't have the right product at the right time, friends are usually really good at helping you out.

If you think that you might find it difficult to buy your own period products, you might be able to ask a parent or caregiver to help you. If they aren't able to, then your school may be able to provide free period products. Some schools are given government funding so that they can support students who need free disposable pads or tampons. Being honest about the support you need can make a massive difference, so speak to a trusted adult, like the school nurse, if you'd like to know more about the options available to you.

● **What other changes are going to happen to me, and how can I find out more about them?**
These are just some of the changes that happen in puberty. What happens to your emotions, your body, your relationships and your life will continue to change, and the questions will keep on coming. You do not need to be an EXPERT in any of this yet. Keep asking questions and use the trusted adults around you if you want to know more. It's like lots of little bits of a puzzle that will all come together when it needs to.

So what's NEXT?

● **Now I know about this stuff, is it OK to tell ALL my friends?**
Nothing in this book is a deep, dark secret. It's great to feel confident about the words and the information. It SHOULD be something you can talk to your friends about, and it SHOULD be something we are all comfortable with, BUT you must also remember to respect *choice* – choices that suit you, your body, your family, your culture, your religion and your personal beliefs. You have to let other families make their own choices about these important topics.

If you are lucky enough to have lots of information and a good understanding, that is great. But it doesn't mean that you are now the teacher and can go and tell everyone else everything. It's a bit like the ending of a fantastic book . . .

It's **NOT** up to you to tell **everyone** in your class. They must find out for themselves in their **OWN WAY**!

Should I keep secrets?

Sometimes secrets are fun and they don't really matter, but some secrets are massive and important, especially if they are something to do with a body or a feeling. If there is something you are worried about, you do not have to keep this a secret. If there is something that has happened and you feel bad about it, you do not have to keep this a secret. If someone has done something you don't feel OK with, you do not have to keep this a secret. There are always trusted adults you can tell, who can help make things better if you just ask.

What if I want to know more about the next bit and then the next bit?

If you really, really, really, really want to know more and if you know a trusted adult who will do the research with you, then we would recommend some of the organizations and websites on page 104 for additional factual, accurate information.

FIND OUT MORE

FOR KIDS

If you want to learn more about any of the topics covered in this book, here are some great organizations that can help:

● Amaze

www.amaze.org

www.amaze.org/jr

Amaze offers fun, animated videos that give you all the answers you want to know about sex, your body and relationships. If you're aged between 4 and 9, visit amaze jr.

● Childline

www.childline.org.uk

0800 1111

Childline is a free and private service for anyone under the age of 19. They have a free 24-hour helpline you can call to talk to a counsellor about anything that's worrying you, or you can get information about feelings, friends, bullying and more on their website.

● Health for Kids

www.healthforkids.co.uk

This NHS website has lots of fun games, articles and activities to help you learn about staying healthy and looking after your health.

● ThinkUKnow

www.thinkuknow.co.uk

ThinkUKnow offers advice about staying safe online when you're on a phone, tablet or computer, as well as advice on what to do if you're worried about something happening online.

DEAR ADULTS

First and foremost, this book is for children.

Children can find out about growing up on their own if that is what is right for them. We explain all of these very **interesting things** about growing up in a **brilliantly simple** way so that they can read this independently.

BUT . . . this book is also for you.

Have you ever been asked a question by a child and haven't known **how** to **respond**?

This book is a toolkit to help you with those moments, and is full of answers to support you when you have these important conversations with a child.

One of us is a nurse, and one of us is a teacher. Together we have delivered lessons to thousands of children and parents about the big topics – including relationships and sex education – that will help equip children for adult life.

With big topics come big questions, and we allow children to ask us anything. This book is made from the **real-life questions** that the **real-life children** we've met have asked us. Children are curious and ask brilliant things all the time. We want to help you feel ready to answer all of these big questions in a way that is right for you and the children you care about, and you can choose to explore these answers together or separately.

Our hope is that this book will inspire lots of honest and comfortable conversations with the children in your life . . . with a few giggles too!

When is the right time to use this book?

You've probably heard of 'the talk' – when an adult decides that it's the right time to sit a child down and tell them about the facts of life.

We all know that this is rarely what happens. Instead there are lots of little chats, conversations and questions that can come, perhaps when a pet dog has puppies, or when someone is breastfeeding in a café, or when people are naked in a swimming-pool changing room.

Everyday situations inspire these questions and it's IMPOSSIBLE to package all of this up for 'the talk'.

Some children will ask questions earlier than others, and you can have great discussions with them at any age. Your three-year-old might be learning to name body parts; your six-year-old might be curious about babies; your eight-year-old might ask about puberty; your ten-year-old might want to talk about privacy. Some children won't be interested until they are older. Some children will hear about these things at school and bring the conversation home. Others will feel very private about it.

Everyone will use this book at different moments. The important thing is responding to your child's lead. The *right* time is when *they* are interested, and when you both feel ready to have these conversations together.

There is a lot of research out there that suggests early sex and relationship education has a positive impact on young people's wellbeing. For many years, the Netherlands has implemented a comprehensive relationship and sex education programme called 'Spring Fever' in primary schools. It is commonplace to start having positive, clear and factually accurate conversations with children from a young age about this important part of their lives. As a result, young people in the Netherlands are confident about naming body parts and understanding concepts like consent. It is no surprise that the Netherlands also has impressive data regarding condom use, and low rates of teenage pregnancies and STIs.

Teaching young children about healthy attitudes to bodies, boundaries and feelings sets them up to protect and care for themselves and others, and helps them go on to form positive relationships as teenagers and adults.

How do I use this book?

Everyone will use this book in different ways. It is important that you find the way that best suits you and the children in your life. Here are our top tips for having the best conversations possible.

DO . . .

- Use correct terminology.
- Reassure children that there is no such thing as 'normal'.
- Explain that there often isn't one right answer, but lots of choices.
- Discuss their options.
- Admit it if you don't know the answer. You can visit a reliable site like www.nhs.uk and look it up together.

- Show children that you are listening and acknowledge it when they make an interesting point. Sometimes the youngest children make the most astute observations, and we can learn from them.

- Use a visual aid to explain. The pictures in this book will help visual learners.

- Keep communication channels open by telling children that you are happy to talk more when they are ready.

TRY NOT TO . . .

- Think that you have to tell a child EVERYTHING at once because they asked you one question.

- Make them feel embarrassed or ashamed. Frame each discussion positively, and remember that there is no such thing as a silly question.

- Stereotype when describing people and relationships – it's important to think carefully about your use of language.

- Leave anyone out. Children will have friends and other people they interact with who have different beliefs about bodies and relationships.

- Feel like you have to disclose personal information. You can if you want to, but privacy is important too. You can always talk about how 'research says something', or about 'some people', or characters in films or on TV, for example.

If in doubt, it's always a good idea to say, 'That is SUCH a good question,' or 'It's OK to want to know about that,' or 'Great questions! Let's chat about it on the way home.' Bide your time. If you don't know the best way to answer the question straight away, you might need to have a think, or talk to friends, family or partners, or do some research.

This is an opportunity to encourage children's curiosity and inspire more brilliant questions about the world. By showing that you are comfortable, you can encourage children to have confidence talking about emotions, relationships, bodies and sex.

You can give them good words. You can tell them that their feelings are valid. You can make it positive. Inclusive. Funny. Joyous.

Because we all want children to feel as CONFIDENT and comfortable about growing up as possible.

Amy & Alex

Amy and Alex

FURTHER INFORMATION

If you are a parent, caregiver, educator, teacher or anyone looking for further helpful resources, you can visit:

FOR ADULTS

Amaze

www.amaze.org

Amaze is an American organization which offers free online animations to help explain topics around sex education for children and adolescents. They also offer content on amaze jr. for younger children aged 4-9.

Department for Education

www.gov.uk

The Department for Education (DfE) is the UK government department responsible for children's services and education, including early years, schools, and higher and further education policy. To read the latest statutory guidance on relationships education and relationships and sex education from the DfE, you can find it on the above website. The new curriculum will be mandatory in all schools from September 2020.

It Happens

www.ithappens.education/
thingswelike

The authors of this book have a section on their website with up-to-date information about books, research, organizations and resources to support you as you continue to have these conversations with the children in your life.

No Outsiders

www.no-outsiders.com

Founded by Andrew Moffat MBE, this organization provides training and resources, such as lesson plans, to educational providers to help promote community cohesion and ideals of tolerance in young children. Their motto is: 'No one is the same – but everyone is equal.'

NSPCC

www.nspcc.org.uk
www.net-aware.org.uk

The charity helps protect children from abuse and cybercrime. Their PANTS campaign is a fun and simple way to explain keeping body parts private and consent. Their Net Aware website explains how to start teaching about online safety, and gives apps age and sensitivity ratings.

NHS

www.nhs.uk
www.healthforkids.co.uk/grownups

The NHS website provides clear information and advice on health, puberty, pregnancy, birth and mental health. Their unique child-focused website, healthforkids.co.uk, is created specially for children and features health advice to help your children grow and flourish. The grown-up area of this website offers advice to parents.

PSHE Association

www.pshe-association.org.uk

The PSHE Association is the national body for personal, social, health and economic (PSHE) education, leading the effort to ensure that every pupil receives high-quality provision and providing training and resources to PSHE educators.

Sex Education Forum

www.sexeducationforum.org.uk

An organization which aims to achieve quality relationships and sex education (RSE) for all children and young people. They offer membership for schools and other educators which serves to connect organizations and individuals with the latest practice and policy information. This is a helpful resource for evidence-based research.

Stonewall

www.stonewall.org.uk

Stonewall provides support and advice to people in the LGBT+ community. It also supports individuals and organizations to work out how they can make a difference for LGBT+ people at work, at home and in their communities, and campaigns for LGBT+ equality.

The Proud Trust

www.theproudtrust.org

The Proud Trust is an organization that helps LGBT+ young people empower themselves through youth groups, national and regional LGBT+ youth work networks, managing the LGBT+ Centre for Manchester, delivering training, running events and campaigns, undertaking research, and creating resources.

ThinkUKnow

www.thinkuknow.co.uk

ThinkUKnow is a free education programme which uses games, videos and more to protect children both online and offline which are appropriate for children and young people aged 4-14+, as well as parents and carers.

GLOSSARY

Adolescent A child who has started puberty and is developing into an adult.

Adoption To legally welcome another person's child into your own family and take care of them as your own child.

Amniotic fluid The liquid that surrounds a foetus inside the pregnant person.

Amniotic sac A bag of liquid that holds the amniotic fluid surrounding the foetus to protect it while it grows.

Asexual (or **Ace**) Someone who does not experience sexual and/or romantic attraction.

Birth parents The person who gave birth to a child, or the person who gave their egg or sperm to make a child. This person might not be the child's legal parent (see: **Adoption**).

Bisexual (or **Bi**) An umbrella term used to describe a romantic and/or sexual attraction towards more than one gender. Bisexual people may describe themselves using one or more of a wide variety of terms including, but not limited to, bisexual, pan and queer.

Blended or patchwork family A family that consists of multiple adults, one child or more that they have had with other partners, and any child or children that they have had together.

Body language The movements or positions of your body that show other people how you are feeling without using words.

Body odour (**BO**) A smell on a person's body that is caused by sweat.

Breast pump A way of collecting breast milk so that it can be stored and used to feed a baby later. Some people prefer hand pumps and others like electric ones.

Breastfeeding Feeding a baby using milk from the breast.

Caesarean section (**C-section**) An operation on a pregnant person to allow the birth of the baby through a cut made in the abdomen. This can be planned or this can happen once the body is already in labour.

Cisgender (or **Cis**) Someone whose gender identity is the same as the biological sex they were given at birth. For example, a person who is called female at birth who identifies as a girl or woman.

Clitoris The clitoris is an important part of the vulva. Whilst only the tip of it is visible at the top of the vulva, it is a much bigger organ. It is very sensitive and is linked with pleasurable feelings.

Coming out LGBT+ telling people about their sexuality and/or gender identity. People can come out whenever they choose. It is up to them.

Consent A mutual agreement between two or more people that allows you or someone else to do something. Everyone involved must be able to make a choice and have their voice heard. Consent cannot be pressured and it can be withdrawn at any time.

Cramps Pains in the womb area experienced by some people during their period.

Counsellor Someone who is trained to listen and guide someone through their problems.

Differences in sex development (DSD) A rare condition when a person is born with internal or external sex organs and/or hormones that may not fit the typical definitions of female or male.

Divorce The legal process of ending a marriage.

Donation This is when someone gives some of their eggs or sperm to another person or couple to use to try and create a baby. A trained fertility doctor usually helps with this process.

Egg An egg is a sex cell produced by a female body in the ovaries that carries information about the person who produced it. If this egg cell is fertilized by a sperm cell, it may develop into an embryo, a foetus and then a baby.

Embryo A small group of cells that grow as a result of a sperm fertilizing an egg. This is called an embryo in its first few weeks of development (see: **Foetus**).

Equal Treating everyone in the same way or allowing everyone to have the same opportunities.

Erection When the penis is temporarily harder and bigger than usual.

Ex-husband, ex-wife or ex-partner The person someone was once married to or in a legal partnership with but is now divorced or separated from.

Expressing A person producing breast milk can collect this milk using a breast pump. Then they can store it, feed it to a baby later or dispose of it.

Fertilization When a sperm and egg join together.

Flow Some people have more period blood than others. The amount of period blood can be referred to as a 'heavy flow' or a 'light flow'.

Foetus If a sperm joins with an egg, those cells may become an embryo. If this embryo grows in the womb for around eight weeks, then we call it a foetus.

Fostering Legally raising a child that is not one's own by birth, sometimes for a limited time.

Gay Refers to a man who has a romantic and/or sexual attraction to other men. Also a generic term for lesbian and gay sexuality – some women define themselves as gay rather than lesbian. Some non-binary people may also identify with this term.

Gender Often expressed in terms of masculinity and femininity, gender is often thought of as culturally and socially determined.

Gender dysphoria A clinical diagnosis used to describe the distress a person can feel if there is a mismatch between the biological sex they were given at birth and their gender identity.

Half-sibling A sibling who has one of the same parents as you do, but whose other parent is different from yours.

Heterosexual (or **Straight**) A person who is sexually attracted to people of the opposite sex.

Homosexual This is a term to describe people who are sexually attracted to people of the same sex. This word is quite old-fashioned and lots of people may prefer to use other terms to describe themselves.

Hormone Naturally produced chemicals in

the body – they control things like growth, development and biological sex.

Identical twins Two people who came from the same fertilized egg, are the same sex and look extremely similar in appearance.

In vitro fertilization (**IVF**) A medical procedure when an egg is fertilized by a sperm outside the body and the embryo is transferred into the womb to continue growing.

Intersex Sometimes people with differences in sex development find the word 'intersex' a helpful way to describe themselves (see: **DSD**).

Labour When the muscles of the womb contract and the cervix opens so that the baby can be born. This process can start spontaneously or with medical help.

Lesbian Refers to a woman who has a romantic and/or sexual attraction towards women. Some non-binary people may also identify with this term.

LGBT+ The acronym for lesbian, gay, bi and trans identities. You might see it with a Q (LGBTQ+), which can mean queer or questioning.

Married To have a wife, husband or legal partner. This usually happens through a ceremony or wedding, and the couple might give each other a ring.

Masturbation The act of touching your own genitals in a way that feels nice. It is very typical for humans to do this and can be a healthy way to learn about your body.

Meconium The first poo a baby does! This poo contains everything that has been in the baby's bowel while it was growing in the womb. It is very dark in colour and looks a bit like tar.

Mental health This is the wellbeing of a person's mind. We all have mental health.

Midwife Someone trained to help deliver babies.

Mindful To be aware of your body, mind and feelings in the present moment, in order to create a feeling of calm. This can improve your mental wellbeing.

Nocturnal emission Also called a wet dream, this is when the penis releases a small amount of semen during the night. This release might be linked to a dream, but not always.

Non-binary An umbrella term for people whose gender identity doesn't sit comfortably with 'man' or 'woman'. Non-binary people may identify with no gender or with more than one gender.

Non-identical twins Two people who grew in the same womb and were born at the same time, but who do not look exactly the same because they developed from two separate eggs.

Overdue A pregnant person is often given a 'due date'. If their baby isn't born before this date, then the baby is considered 'late' or 'overdue'.

Ovulate The release of an egg from the ovary down into the fallopian tube. This release, called ovulation, only happens once a body has gone through puberty. It varies from person to person, but ovulation tends to happen about once a month.

Penis External genitals of male mammals – used for passing urine (wee) and having sex. This organ is very sensitive and is also linked with pleasurable feelings.

Period Once ovulation happens, the womb

lining thickens. If the egg isn't fertilized, the womb lining is released and a small about of menstrual blood comes out of the vagina. The release of this womb lining as menstrual blood is called a period.

Placenta This organ develops inside the uterus during pregnancy and provides oxygen and nutrients for the growing baby through the umbilical cord. Once the baby is born, the placenta leaves the pregnant person's body.

'Plus' or '+' symbol A term which can incorporate or reject specific labels regarding sexuality, gender and sex.

Pregnant To have an embryo, foetus or baby inside the womb.

Premature birth When a baby is born three or more weeks before the due date given.

Pronouns The words we use to refer to people's gender - for example, 'he', 'she' or 'they'.

Puberty A set of changes that happen to the body of a child as it becomes an adult body. These changes can include hair and body growth, and may mean that reproduction is possible one day.

Pubic hair Pubic hair is the hair around the genital area of adolescents and adults, located around the sex organs (penis and vagina). It is there to cushion and protect these body parts.

Queer A term used by those wanting to reject specific labels of romantic attraction, sexual attraction and/or gender identity.

Questioning A person who is uncertain about and/or exploring their own sexual attraction and/or gender identity.

Reproduction The process of parents producing children and therefore a species continuing to grow.

Scrotum A part of the male reproductive system made up of a sack of skin that contains the testicles.

Semen A sticky, creamy liquid containing millions of sperm.

Separating When couples stop living together or no longer see themselves as a couple.

Sex (biological) The biological sex of a person assigned at birth based on characteristics like genitals (for example, females have a vulva and

males have a penis). Sex is not limited to either male or female because there are also other identities such as DSD (see: **DSD**).

Sex Refers to the many different ways people use their genitals and bodies to connect with each other in a way that feels nice or is pleasurable.

Sexual intercourse Usually used to describe when a penis goes inside a vagina. This can sometimes result in the sperm fertilizing the egg but not always.

Single-use plastic Disposable plastic that's designed to be used once and then thrown away, recycled or destroyed.

Social workers Social workers are professionals who support adults, children, families and communities to help them with their lives.

Sperm A sperm is a sex cell produced in the male body carrying information about the person who produced it. Millions of sperm are found in semen. Sperm can swim and have the ability to fertilize an egg.

Stepbrother or stepsister If you have a stepmother or stepfather, and if that person already has children from a previous relationship, then those children become your stepbrothers and stepsisters.

Stepmother or stepfather A person who is married to someone's parent but who is not their birth parent.

Stereotype A fixed idea that people have about what someone or something is like. This is often based on assumption and myth.

Straight See: **Heterosexual**.

Surrogate parent Someone who voluntarily grows a baby in their womb and gives birth to it for another person or couple.

Testicles (**testes**) Usually two round male sex organs that produce sperm and are enclosed in the scrotum behind the penis.

Transgender (**trans**) An umbrella term to describe people whose gender identity does not sit comfortably with the biological sex they were given at birth.

Ultrasound image Using ultrasound scanning technology, a specialist can capture an image of the growing foetus or baby inside the womb.

Umbilical cord The tube that connects a baby in the womb to the pregnant person, and carries oxygen and nutrients to it through the placenta.

Vagina The vagina is a reproductive internal female organ. It is a tube that leads from the womb to the vaginal entrance.

Vaginal discharge A small amount of clear or white fluid released from the vagina. As with other self-cleaning organs, this bodily fluid is natural and healthy, just like noses have bogeys and ears have earwax!

Vocal cords Muscles which are stretched across the voice box, a bit like rubber bands, and vibrate when a person speaks. They lengthen and thicken during puberty, making the voice deeper. This change happens to both girls and boys, but can be much more noticeable in boys.

Voice box or **larynx** This is located in the throat and works with the vocal cords to create the sound of a voice. It grows larger and thicker during puberty.

Vulva The vulva is the external female genitals. It is on the outside of the body. It includes the vaginal opening, the urethra, labia and the clitoris.

Wet dream See: **Nocturnal emission**.

Womb (**uterus**) The organ inside the abdomen where an embryo, foetus and baby develops before it is born. It is connected to the cervix and the vaginal entrance. It is not in the stomach.

The **words** people use are very personal and can **CHANGE** over time, so please visit the **websites** listed on pages 110–111 for the most up-to-date **terminology**.

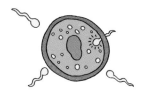 # INDEX

ABOUT THE AUTHORS

Amy (MPhil PGCE) studied in Bristol and now lives near Hay-on-Wye (which has lots of brilliant books in it). Amy has worked in many educational settings over the years: she has run exciting **community projects**, has done **youth work**, and is a **qualified teacher** and **school governor**.

When she isn't walking up mountains or doing yoga, she mostly reads non-fiction and **academic research**, and goes to many **conferences**. Amy spends a lot of her time in schools all over the UK **supporting students, teachers and parents to untangle some of the trickiest taboos**.

Alex is a **registered nurse** and has worked in a variety of medical settings over the years. Her biggest passion and specialist field is working in **sexual health and contraception**, specifically with teenagers and their families.

When she isn't riding her bike or looking after her animals, she spends her time in UK schools, colleges and the community making sure everyone knows about the **amazing NHS** and **other organizations that are there to support children and teenagers with relationships and intimacy**.

Amy and Alex both have families of their own, love telling stories and really like to giggle too. **Together, they founded It Happens Education and they, and the whole team, really believe that a bit of kindness, accuracy and honesty can keep everyone safer, healthier and ultimately happier**!

Thank you to all of the children, students, and parents who have asked us brilliant questions. We couldn't have written this book without you!